LIVING WITH ASPERGERS: DANIEL'S STORY

By

Daniel Jones

I'd Like To Dedicate My Book To:

My Mum, Catherine

My Dad, Kevin

My Sister, Charlotte

My Brother In Law, Jack

My Brother's Aaron, Thomas & Harry

My Sister In Law, Kayleigh

My Niece, Millie

My Best Friend's Alex, Richard & Bea

My Online Community

I call them,

FAMILY

Living With Aspergers: Daniel's Story by Daniel Jones

Published by Daniel Jones

https://livingwithdan.com/

Copyright © 2022 Daniel Jones

All rights reserved. No portion of this book may be reproduced in any form without permission from the publisher, except as permitted by U.K. copyright law. For permissions contact: Daniel Jones.

Cover by Daniel Jones

CONTENTS

BLOG EXTRACT: AUTISM IS A TALENT NOT A DISABILTY   12

BIRTH   22

BLOGGING   28

BLOG EXTRACT: WHY I RUN   30

EDUCATION   32

BLOG EXTRACT: COPING WITH MY CAR ACCIDENT   40

MY BEDROOM   43

BLOG EXTRACT: HOW I STARTED RUNNING   48

TALKING   50

BLOG EXTRACT: READY TO RUN SILVERSTONE   54

MUSIC   55

ORGANISATION	57
BLOG EXTRACT: HOW RUNNING CHANGED MY LIFE	62
ASTHMA	65
TECHNOLOGY	67
TRANSPORT	69
BLOG EXTRACT: THE NATIONAL RUNNING SHOW #BESTDAYEVER	72
FUNDRAISING	74
BLOG EXTRACT: THE REAL REASON I RUN	79
DRAMA	81
FINDING LOVE	85
WEATHER	90
TELEVISION	92

MARATHONS	**96**
BLOG EXTRACT: WHAT IF YOU WERE TOLD "YOU CAN'T EXERCISE FOR 30 DAYS"?	**99**
WATER	**101**
GYM	**103**
RELIGION	**105**
BLOG EXTRACT: BELIEVE YOU CAN AND YOU WILL	**107**
FOOD	**111**
BLOG EXTRACT: A LETTER TO AN 18 YEAR OLD DAN	**120**
NANNY AND GRAMPY	**123**
WORK	**128**
THEME PARKS	**134**
RUNNING	**138**

TWITTER	**140**
RUN TALK RUN	**141**
BLOG EXTRACT: MY FIRST RUN TALK RUN	**143**
HOLIDAYS	**145**
THOUGHTS DIARY	**159**
ONE YEAR LATER	**175**

INTRO

If you don't know me, my name is Daniel 'Edwin' Jones (I'm not a big fan of the name 'Edwin', oh well, that's what it says on my passport). Currently, I'm 30 years old, I have a car, I have a passion for running, I wrote my own blog, runningwithdan.com, it's now called livingwithdan.com, in case you haven't come across my blog before I have kindly inserted extracts from my blog within this book, and of course I have Aspergers/ High Functioning Autism and OCD.

So, What is Aspergers?

According to the Oxford English Dictionary, Aspergers has been defined as:

"A neurodevelopmental disorder characterized by significant difficulties in social interaction and nonverbal communication, along with restricted and repetitive patterns of behaviour and interests."

Now you're probably thinking, "what on earth does 'neurodevelopmental' mean?", I know I am. So let's break it down, to put it simply, Aspergers to me means you struggle to communicate verbally, i.e in social situations and you struggle to communicate non verbally i.e within your body language. Basically it means you struggle to communicate and understand the world we live in today, you struggle to understand why people even talk, what people actually talk about and how to even talk yourself. You struggle to understand people's thoughts, feelings and emotions and how to address them in the everyday world. You struggle to do simply things like go into a shop and buy a tin of baked beans, don't know why I'd choose baked beans, I'd probably prefer the chocolate but anyway, it's that kind of thing. At parties, you'll be the one standing around wondering what to do. Imagine, waking up one morning and having to think of every word, emotion and feeling you say and do.

Of course over time you become more and more confident in expressing these feelings, emotions and body language and that's what life has been like for me, once I get to know someone I become like a whole new person. Of course this is different for everyone, having Aspergers or a form of autism is hard for everyone but in different ways. Some people don't struggle with the social side, but the thing is I'm not looking at Aspergers as a Doctor, I'm looking at the diagnoses from my perspective and that's the shy me, the person who wouldn't even go into a shop on their own 10 years ago, the person who struggles to make friends because it's so blimin hard to get a conversation together, the person who probably won't get married, have kids or have a girlfriend because socially I struggle and I'm not afraid to admit that because that's my disability.

"I Have To Think About Every Single Word When I Talk."

Of course, it's not all negative having Aspergers, there are plenty of positives too, for example if you put your mind to something, you can be anything you want to be. That's one common trait upon people with Aspergers, if they put their minds to something, they can achieve it. As it said in the quote at the start of this book, having Aspergers means you gain "restricted and repetitive behaviours" which means if you become focused on a task you love repeating it and repeating it until you perfect it and that's one positive that I can relate to. Take my running for example, I run and run and run until I achieved an average time of 7.30 minutes per mile. I ran the London Marathon in 3 hours 44 minutes but I pushed myself more and more and more until I became ill, yes ill and you'll find out more about that later on in this book.

Anyway, moving on, just have a look at the amount of famous people who've been diagnosed with Aspergers, Albert Einstein, Isaac Newton and many, many more, all had a form of autism, that's because they focused on their talent and kept going until they were successful.

"If You Put Your Mind To Something You Can Do It."

BLOG EXTRACT: AUTISM IS A TALENT NOT A DISABILTY

Albert Einstein, Isaac Newton, Steve Jobs, Bill Gates, Hans Christian Andersen, Charles Darwin, Michelangelo and many, many others have one common trait. They all had a form of ASPERGERS or AUTISM. Before you read this blog, I bet you didn't know that, I bet you're wondering how on earth they accomplished so much with such a disadvantage, well they didn't have a disadvantage they had a talent, a talent nobody sees but them and me, as I have Aspergers and I know how they think, they think different and it's this difference that makes me and them so amazing and running makes this difference even more amazing.

Focus

I have the most incredibly ability to focus, when I run I can focus in on my objective whatever distance that maybe, a marathon, half marathon or dare I say it, ultra marathon. This focus means I can get a task done without being distracted, in the workplace, for example, I can sit in the office all day with no music just the focus and drive to succeed and get a task done without having to talk about nonsense. I can run on the treadmill with no music, nothing, just the sound of steps pattering away. I don't get bored, I don't lose focus, I don't drift off, it's this focus that's made me who I am today. I went to University, I wrote my dissertation before the end of October, that's a 10,000 word essay by the way, it wasn't due until May the following year. Focus and success, it's one common trait amongst us with autism and it's something not many people see.

Organisation

If you want to know what real organisation is, look no further than me. I work Monday to Friday 9am to 5pm, commute an hour a day and still find time to go to the gym twice a week, run several runs a week, set up this blog which by the way I'm writing now, launch my own running grou, manage a car insurance claim, strength train every morning, watch TV and sleep. How on earth do I do it? ORGANISATION! I know what I'm doing tomorrow, the next and the next day. Tomorrow's Saturday, so I'm running a long run in the morning, hoovering the house, getting the shopping in, visiting my Nan and then watching Ant and Dec's Saturday Night Takeaway!

"Listen to me, Aspergers or autism for that matter is a talent, we're being told we have a disability, a weakness, *we can't do things other people can, it's RUBBISH, we have a talent, use it and the MAGIC will happen!"*

I'm aware my blog's becoming a book so I'll start to conclude, might just have to think about writing one, HINT, HINT. Having Aspergers makes it extremely difficult when it comes to new challenges; one thing that's helped me is running. Running's given me so much more confidence, as I've said before I organised my own raffle last year, I've just started using the phone at work and I really feel it's made me a whole new person. If you're reading this with Aspergers and you're feeling down and wondering why you are on this earth, listen to me. Aspergers or autism for that matter is a talent, we're being told we have a disability, a weakness, we can't do things other people can, it's RUBBISH, we have a talent, use it and the MAGIC will happen!

Anyway, moving on, I'm sat here writing my book in a psychiatric ward in a mental health hospital after becoming ill, yes my repeated behaviours or in other words my running got the better of me and I ended up having a psychotic episode. I know what you're thinking, how can someone with such a strong routine, job and structure, collapse and end up with almost everything taken away from them, for good reasons of course. The truth is, everyone has a weakness but I'm using this experience to learn from my mistakes, I thoroughly believe you can learn new things from every life experience you have, you can learn new skills every day and take the positives from them rather than the negatives. That's the reason I'm sat here writing this book because I don't want to sit around in this mental health hospital and give up, I want to learn from this experience, I want something to come out of this hard time in my life and that's why I'm going to take you through my life throughout this book, this is my story, this is Daniel Jones story.

"You can learn new things from every life experience."

So, "what caused my psychotic episode?". A year ago I would have never thought I'd be in this hospital but then all of a sudden, my life changed due to coronavirus, I had to work from home. I know what you're thinking, "what is coronavirus and what's the big deal about working from home?". Coronavirus is essentially a killer disease that's closed the whole WORLD down, making it five times more harder for people like me with Aspergers, with autism to focus and control there life. Without structure and control, someone with Aspergers might struggle. I especially struggle with change, I need routine in my life and the pressure and change of coronavirus as well as working from home essentially led to my psychotic episode.

"The WHOLE WORLD has closed down."

Anyway, after not too long I started seeing clowns telling me to do stuff I would have never dreamed of doing. Things like "kill myself, my Mum and my family". This was a scary time for me, I remember going for a walk and walking past a shop window and seeing the clown waving at me. I remember sitting on the sofa and seeing the clown underneath my feet. I remember going to do lunch and not being able to pick up a knife because I was too frightened I'd do something.

I went to the hospital and they said to ignore the clowns, how can you ignore the clown I was seeing every moment. I wasn't sleeping either and was talking to myself and hearing a voice, ironically called Dan inside my head. At night, Dan was talking to me saying I was a "true inspiration" and saying I could do "anything". Gradually these voices got stronger and stronger before I started going into trances and I couldn't cope. I spent several nights in a trance with my brain telling me that I'd cured my Aspergers, that mindfulness is the way forward in life, that we should appreciate everything on the planet. I remember going for a bath the night before going into hospital and hallucinating the bath rising and flooding the bathroom. I remember me hearing things throughout the night, it was a really scary time for me. It literally was like living in a nightmare.

Although these trances were good, I shouldn't have been having them, they were all about running and being positive but they were giving me a false representation of life. Then my Mum split up with her boyfriend, I'm not blaming her for my collapse but it did mean I had to go and live with my Dad. I needed help and I'm glad to say I know have it and I'm recovering well.

Ultimately, my psychotic episode was all about being a positive person and I promote this on my blog that "anything is possible", you can do anything but there are also negative things in life.

"It Was Like Living In A Nightmare."

After arriving at hospital, my brain started thinking of an escape route as I was in a Psychiatric ward so I started telling myself that these people (the nurses) were cyborgs and weren't real, I was telling myself I was the cure for coronavirus, that I was superhuman. This is really hard for me write at the moment but I now realise that those thoughts I was having weren't real, they were all imaginary but the thoughts come from my brain and the pressure and stress I was under. This was mainly because of coronavirus alongside burning out by setting myself high targets through running and exercise.

So let me talk a bit more about coronavirus. Coronavirus is a disease that's caused the whole world to be put on standby. Business after business has collapsed because of the disease. If you're reading this in the distant future, give coronavirus a Google and you'll see the devastation it's caused. Football matches have stopped, pubs have shut, shops are closed, no one can go out except for one bit of exercise a day or for essential grocery shops. If you visit a shop it can take an hour to get in, you have to maintain a distance of at least 2 metres apart and wear a mask like you're some kind of Doctor. It's almost like living in a zombie world. It's literally like living in a scene from The Walking Dead, if you see someone out on the street you literally have to jump out their way. The world is in complete lockdown, you literally cannot do anything and that's the reason I'm writing this in a Psychiatric ward because my Aspergers brain wasn't set in structure.

Coronavirus wasn't the only thing that's caused my breakdown; Aspergers is so set on structure and it's something you'll notice as I write this book, how my structure is the element to my life, I like to do things in certain ways. For example, my day has to have structure in it; I wake up, have Breakfast, exercise, work, eat then sleep. If I don't have structure I get panicky and don't know what to think. This structure has resulted in myself getting burnout, I put too much pressure on myself to perform almost at an elite level in running. I was at the gym twice a week, I ran four times a week, I worked 9am to 5pm, I barely had any time for relaxation and taking care of myself. That's why it's changing from today that being (Saturday 30th May), if I don't want to do something I don't have to, I can enjoy life, eat what I want, of course within limits and exercise when I want to, not when my brain says you should. When I choose to do something, I need to start thinking in my mind "do I want to do this?" and if I do, I need to go and do it but then pack away as soon as I start getting too stressed over the situation. Of course with things like work this cannot always be the way forward but that's why I am in this hospital, to get better to prepare me for highly stressful situations.

To tell you the truth, I've never suffered with anxiety this bad, but as I've said previously, it's due to coronavirus. My Mum suffers with anxiety terribly too, she was taken to hospital not long ago and she thought she'd never walk again but I'm glad to say she is walking now, she's even ran more than me whilst I'm in hospital.

"I put too much pressure on myself, to perform almost at an elite level."

I'm sat here writing this now, I'm thinking about my big project, that big project being writing this book, writing this book to help and inspire those with Aspergers that they can live a good life, that they are talented, after all as I've written on my blog, Aspergers is a gift, it's a talent and it's something I want to make people aware of within this book. Whilst being a gift it can mean you put yourself under high stress and you end up breaking just as I have.

Being in this psychiatric ward has really messed my structure up, which is a good thing of course. I don't have everything I need but I'm slowly getting it back. My structure in my ward begins with Breakfast, then I go to do a workout in my bedroom, I put the radio on, I like a bit of background music. After Breakfast I'm now focusing on writing my book, so I head to the Activity Room to write it, I'm also reading a lot to get an idea of what a book structure is like. Aside from my book I've taken up colouring and Kriss Kross, puzzle books really get the brain thinking and that's something I really need to focus on, staying focused on a task. As well as being focused, staying relaxed is also key, just simply lying down on my bed and just thinking. I've thought of some amazing thoughts to do with this book, you'll read them throughout.

BIRTH

Let's start at the beginning shall we, the moment you're born, it's not a quiet affair that's for sure, continuous screams, blood pouring out from under the umbilical cord, gulps of oxygen being consumed from the pregnant Mother. I mean luckily I didn't see any of that when I was born, as I was the one actually being born.

Ultimately, it's such a special time when you're born, you're new to this massive open world. When I was born I weighed, well I'm not sure really how much I weighed I'll have to ask my Mum, I know for definite I was a boy, a male and I was a baby, a healthy baby. My Mum still has my Birth Certificate, I must get it off her actually, it's such an important document, I must keep it close to me. Anyway, when you're born, not that I can remember being born if I did I would be a top mind reading illusionist, but anyway when you're born you appreciate the small things in life, like food, like your parents, like clothes, like every single little bit of feeling.

"It's important to appreciate the small things in life."

That's exactly what I'm going through now being in this mental health hospital, I'm appreciating such small things in my life, like meal times, like being able to write this book using my laptop, like using my phone. It's such small things but I've never been so grateful for them and it's exactly the same principle when you're born. Being sat here writing this book in a mental health hospital is hard, I'm clock watching all the time, I'm sitting on a bed counting the minutes and hours until I can go home but I know I'm not ready just yet. As I sit here and write this, it's like being reborn again, reborn into the world and appreciating the small things you do.

The capitalist society we live in today is all about making money, about material goods but what if we were left with nothing but you. That's why being born is so special because it's you entering the world as you, you're not being defined by TV, by advertising, by the media, it's YOU, you as a baby, being left to define YOU as a person.

So, what does it mean to be on the planet? Well, it means everything, being born here on earth with other people. When I had my psychotic episode I really thought I was dead and this was the end of life, I really thought that I was in heaven and that was it. See, my psychotic episode made me think I was dead but I was reborn but the only way out was to code the cyborgs to let me out the building. I really thought I was going to be held captive for the rest of my life. That feeling is horrible, it's not nice and it's kind of why I treasure every day from now on.

"What am I going to do on the planet?"

What I am going to do on the planet? That's the question I need to ask myself now. I appreciate so much being on this planet, I mean if my Mum hadn't met my Dad then I wouldn't be here now, obviously. There's so much I can do the planet too, I'm learning Spanish using an app called Duolingo, that's really working well, I'm really advancing my knowledge of Spanish each day, simply by logging on and answering a few daily trivia questions in relation to Spanish. I'm going to run another marathon again, yes I am going to do this, but it has to be when the time is right. I'm not going to come out of hospital and run 20 miles, I need to rest and recover.

In terms of my blogging, I'm starting it up again. I've re-designed my blog, it's now called livingwithdan.com as it's all about appreciating the small things in life and the way we live. That reminds me, I must get a new blog on my site today, a new blog to kick start my blogging again. Anyway, there's so much for me living on this planet, being born on this planet, there's running, there's blogging, there's my MIND group who have been so supportive. I'll go into them later on in this book, anyway, being born on this planet means everything to me.

In terms of the birth experience, I've had three experiences of birth really and that was when my younger brothers, Thomas and Harry and my niece, Millie were born. I remember handling Thomas, Harry and Millie my niece for the first time as they entered the world. It was incredible; it gave me such a good, fuzzy feeling inside. It was a magical time, seeing new life being brought into the world, new babies are like a bundle of joy but they grow up so fast.

Babies are so innocent when they arrive on the planet, they haven't done anything wrong. I remember when Thomas was born, he tried to take my glasses off me, the little monkey, he must have been thinking "What are these? Can I touch them?", of course in my mind I'm thinking, "don't touch them, you'll break them" but babies are unaware of the dangers and stress of everyday life. Thomas didn't realise that if he were to break my glasses I wouldn't be able to see for a while until they are repaired at Specsavers (other shops selling glasses are available, of course you should go to Specsavers). On the other hand, Harry didn't try and take my glasses as I was prepared and removed my glasses before handling Harry as a baby. I like to think that someday I would leave a child in the world before I die. Of course, finding love is so difficult with my Aspergers and it's something I talk about later on in this book.

"I belong to a large group of siblings."

In terms of siblings, I belong to a large family, there's me, Daniel, born on the 23rd December, then there's Charlotte, my sister, the second eldest, then there's my brother Aaron, and my two younger brothers, Thomas and Harry. I don't feel any pressure being the eldest of the family, in fact, sorry to be a bit biased I've been the most successful, well I like to think I have, I like to think this is because of my Aspergers. The thing is, what is success? I mean I've got a degree, I have a good and steady job that I enjoy and I have the most wonderful family in the world, isn't that success?

If I have to look back, my earliest memory probably would be going to Nursery. I kind of remember my Mum saying to me "go on, you'll be okay" as I walked into Nursery not knowing what to expect. That's my first sign of independence, although obviously there were teachers there to help me. I think nursery is your first sign of being independent as a child, I know you have the teachers but you still have to think independently and be you. Having Aspergers, thinking can often get too much especially when you're on your own and having to make decisions by yourself. That's why it's so difficult living with Aspergers because your brain is processing thought, time and time again, that's why structure and knowing what you're doing at a specific time is so crucial.

BLOGGING

Honestly, I'm so glad I set up my blog, it's inspired so many people to run and exercise. I know I've re-designed it now to livingwithdan.com but If you're reading this now and you've been inspired to start running or exercise please let me know, I'd love to hear all about your journey and how you've been reading my blog. We can maybe do a piece on your journey for my blog. I'm so keen to make my blog huge, this came across in my psychotic episode as I thought I had died and been reborn but the blog had gone viral whilst I was dead. This was my imagination but it just shows how I'm so keen to share my story and influence others to take up running or a lose weight or conquer there Aspergers or High Functioning Autism.

"I love blogging."

The question I have to ask myself though, is "why did I start my blog?", why did an ordinary runner like me start writing about running and things you can do to help you run. To tell you the truth, I wanted to be bigger than Runners World, I wanted to have advert after advert embedded within the blog, the truth is though, I still can do this, I can still make runningwithdan.com bigger than

Runners World. I just need to start writing a lot more on my blog.

I have to admit though, when I first started writing my blog, I wanted to make it really commercial, I wanted to make money out of it, but I realise now that's not what it's for. It's a place people can go to be inspired by me. Obviously, I'm not writing any blogs at the minute, but I will be in the near future, at the minute my full focus is writing this book. So if you've missed my blogs, don't worry this one billion word book can be read instead.

BLOG EXTRACT: WHY I RUN

It's now November 2019, I've run Leamington Half Marathon twice, Oxford Half Marathon, Portsmouth's Great South Run, the Vitality Big Half in London, London Marathon, Bournemouth Marathon and I'm sat here with two days to go until I run Silverstone Half Marathon and I'm doing Liverpool Marathon in 2020. But why do I want to keep running?

Believe it or not, back in October 2017, I weighed 18 stone and was severely overweight. I was sat in a Bingo hall one evening, bored as anything, wondering what to do. Then suddenly my brain clicked, you know want, I'll enter Portsmouth's Great South Run. Now being 18 stone and having not run in five and a bit years, you might be thinking why I am even considering entering a run, and this was not just a run, this was 10 miles.

So, that was it, I was signed up, I had eight months to train for a 10 mile run around Portsmouth. Now, I'm not going to detail all my runs and how I train, that will be in other posts, but what I am going to do is explain why I run and hopefully encourage you to start.

Okay, imagine you're in control of an aircraft, you haven't got a clue how to land, all you can do is fly, fly and fly. That's running, except the aircraft is you. Running allows you to benefit mentally as well as physically. It gives me a chance to leave all my worries at home and just focus on running. Breathing in that fresh air, it's incredible, the scenery, the early mornings and plus you can eat anything you want after.

HOW TO START

Right, it's easy, run. Anyone can do it, it's all in your mind. To begin with, start with a mile, if that's too much, half a mile. I recommend running as far as you can as soon as possible. Wake up one morning and think "I'm going to run 8 miles this morning" and just do it, it really is as simple as it sounds. Tell your brain you can do this. As I have Aspergers, i could quite easily do this, if I'm going to do something, I will. That's how I'm sat here having lost six stone with two days to go until I run my seventh race in three years.

By the way, once you start running, you'll never stop. It's like the BEST DRUG YOU'LL EVER TAKE!

EDUCATION

My education's been very successful. I started at Nursery, then I advanced to Primary School, before going to Blessed George Napier Secondary School. Then I went to college and completed A Levels in History, Media and Drama before moving to Coventry to complete a degree in Communication, Culture and Media at Coventry University where I was extremely successful and achieved an Upper Second Class degree, I was so close to a first class degree. I remember my teacher saying in a Parents Evening that I was capable of achieving much higher grades than I was predicted and I certainly have achieved them. I got over 10 GCSE's, several C's and even a few B's in History and English Literature, I call that a result.

> "You are capable of achieving more than you expect."

Socially, my school days were difficult, I'm not afraid to admit I was bullied throughout my times at school but that didn't stop me being successful in school. I remember being filmed and put on YouTube after a pupil decided to chase me across the school grounds, my Mum reported them and the video footage was taken down. I also had the micky taken out of me for speaking in a high voice. Most of my bullying was verbal abuse but I just ignored it and carried on with my school days. I think if you have Aspergers and are bullied you should just ignore it, you are twice as intelligent as the bullies are. Believe me, the majority of my school bullies are in a low paid job know whilst I am thriving working in a fun and enjoyable job and career. Not to say that there is anything wrong with being in a low paid job. Basically what I'm trying to say is if you keep your head down and ignore them and get on with life, you're more likely to succeed.

"Don't let the bullies dictate your future."

Bullying is so prevalent in schools especially if you're suffering with autism, if you're reading this with autism now and you're getting bullied in school or your child is, I'd say to report it to a Head Teacher but make sure your child is aware to ignore it and carry on with their life. If it's physical abuse then I'd say to move schools or get the bullies reported immediately as this is unacceptable. Throughout my whole education I didn't know I had Aspergers, I was living my life without knowing what was wrong with me, I knew I had OCD but the psychiatrist I saw said there was "no way on earth he has Aspergers". I was only diagnosed at 18 years old just before I was heading to University, but I've continually found a way to combat my disability.

I'm glad to say I did have one friend whilst I was at school, his name was Chris. Me and Chris got on well, we bonded through football and through are similar likes. I've not really been in touch with Chris lately though; I think as we've got older we've kind of gone our own separate ways. When I get out of this mental health hospital, I'm going to get back in touch with Chris and see if he wants to go for a drink. Other than Chris, I did have Robbie. Robbie lived down the road from me and we used to go and play with him. I remember getting our bikes and playing pretend Formula One races on a closed shopping car park near our house, that was a good time using our imagination. Chris and Robbie and a few side friends were pretty much my friend list when I was younger.

"I was petrified, I really didn't want to go and be away from my parents."

I remember when we went on a school trip to Austria. It was in Year 6 of primary school and it was my first time being away from the house. I was petrified, I really didn't want to go and be away from my parents for so long. I remember thoughts racing round in my head, "I wouldn't know anyone in Austria", "They speak German in Austria, German, I don't know a word of German". So I decided to stay put in the car, there was no way I was going on holiday and live with a few of my school friends for a whole week. I remember my Mum and Dad shouting at me as I was kicking and screaming in total panic.

I look back at that moment now and thank my parents for doing that, I know it's hard sending your child away having no clue what to expect but I remember the whole holiday right now, 20 or so years later. It was my first time being abroad and it was amazing. We travelled to Austria all the way by coach, I'm glad to say I wasn't kicking and screaming for 20 or so hours on a coach. I sat next to my best friend Chris who was my friend throughout my school years. I remember when we first arrived in Austria, the scenery was incredible, everywhere you looked there was mountains filled with snow, thick, white snowy mountains across the whole landscape. I'd never seen anything like this before.

That was just the start of our adventure in Austria, we visited the top of a skilling mountain which was incredible. We went up by cable car to the top of a mountain and we had the chance to play in the snow. This snow was so smooth and silky; you could build anything you wanted to out of it. We stopped in a cabin in the woods, I remember going for a walk one evening, one teacher said to me "I'll race you back to the hotel, if you get there first, I'll give you a lollipop.". I did, get there first and I did get a lollipop.

"I had very little support at school, I learnt it all myself."

Taking my GCSE's and A Levels was pretty difficult for me especially as I had very little support. In terms of revising, I pretty much remembered my whole syllabus at school, especially the events in History. I have a very good memory as you'll read later, this memory comes in useful a lot of the time especially when you have to remember a long script like I did in Drama.

Anyway, moving back on to my education, I remember the day I went and collected my GSCE results, my Mum came with me and I was so nervous. We opened the paper and we were delighted, so we decided to go for a meal to celebrate afterwards, me, my Mum and my siblings. After my education at secondary school, I felt I needed to be a bit more independent so I went to college. I studied 3 A Levels in History, Drama and Media Studies. I wasn't just awarded them, I had to work hard for them. If you ask my parents, they'd say I spent more time at home than at college. I'm pleased to say I did make a friend at college, his name was Jeremy, he had a big, black bushy beard, he was pretty clever too. The classes at college were quite small which made it easier to make friends. The maximum size of a class at college was about 15 which really helped as we often had one to one time throughout lessons.

"University made me who I am today."

My University days were amazing; I lived in the same room/ flat on the 18th floor for 3 years. The staff at Coventry University were so good to me, they let me live in the same flat for three years as they knew I'd struggle making friends and go to move into rental accommodation. The flat was on the 18th floor, I could see the whole of Coventry from the top of my flat. Literally, I had an amazing view; it was particular pretty when it was Bonfire Night as I could see all the fireworks going off one by one. Christmas was a special time as I could see all the houses lit up. The flat was small but it was on an ensuite which meant I had a shower and a toilet I could use. That was my living arrangements whilst I was at Coventry, I'd like to say a big thank you to the disability team at Coventry who really helped me and I'm sure have helped others with their mental health.

That was my living arrangements sorted; in terms of planning my days whilst I was at Coventry University I had an adventure. I remember my first Fresher's Week, that was one wild, adventure. I remember going to the local student union bar and it being sports teams' night. I met the Netball Team, there were several girls who were so drunk. They played a drinking game that night, they all lied down and have to down one pint, after the other. That was one weird night but I was so pleased of myself for going. That's my life see, I'm always pushing myself to do things no matter how difficult they may seem.

Other adventures from Freshers Week included going on a bar crawl across Coventry, I had a few ciders that night, not too many though. I also saw a magic act one night who were from Britain's Got Talent and I also attended a Comedy Club which I continued to attend often on a Sunday night. I made a friend at University, he was called Toby. I actually made friends with him on a Disability taster session I attended before I went to University. This was a fantastic idea as it brought together those who were disabled before we went to University to get them used to their surroundings, and it really helped me settle in.

"I couldn't believe the nights I saw on Fresher's Week."

I really become a lot more confident whilst studying for my degree, I often took charge of team meetings as a lot of my course was group based; I spent regular time working with the Media Production students on various media projects. I remember filming a video with clips from different movies, this video saw me dressed as a Ghostbuster in white overalls. Other stuff I had to do whilst studying for my degree included managing a press conference scene at University, I had to work closely with a team to come up with a good portrayal of a fake company. I had to give presentations every week too which really increased my confidence. University literally made me so much more confident as a person and I'm glad to say made me the person that's writing this today.

BLOG EXTRACT: COPING WITH MY CAR ACCIDENT

Being whipped from behind by a car travelling 45mph whilst you're stationary isn't pretty and it damaged me mentally having Aspergers as well as physically, but the good news is that running helped me survive!

The Impact

I knew as soon as that car hit me this was going to be a challenge, having Aspergers Syndrome, I knew this was going to be difficult, all sorts questions started to buzz in my head, "How was I going to get home?", "How was I going to get my car moved?", "How will I get to work in the morning?", "Do I need to pay for another car?", "WHAT DO I DO?". Okay, so I may be thinking these questions but what I've learnt from running and exercise in particular is at times of challenge, always keep calm, you can only face a challenge one step at a time whether it be a car accident or a marathon. So I did exactly that, whilst battling a ton of body shock may I add, which is only natural when a car the weight of an elephant decides to slam in your back of you. First thing I thought; phone my insurance, so I did that.

The Next Day

I've never took so many phone calls in all my life, phone call here, there and everywhere. I hate phone calls, but I know I can do them, as I've said #anythingispossible it's just a matter of putting your mind to it. Now as I've explained before, running has given me no end of confidence and I'm pleased to say this confidence shone through in my handling of my accident. I had GAP insurance so I knew I was able to get a replacement car, it was just a matter of taking calls from Fred, George and Joe Blogs. The first thing I had to do was get a hire car.

Getting A Hire Car

I thought it would be simple, it wasn't, they had to talk to the third party who had to admit liability for me to get a hire car. It was Sunday afternoon, I had to go to work the next day, I needed a hire car so I could get to work but I didn't panic. I had ran a long run the day before so I had time to reset my brain, whilst I was running I was able to draw out a plan of what I needed to do in my head that is, I didn't physically get a pen and start drawing whilst running 20 miles, I would be skilled if I did that. Anyway, back to the story, it was Sunday afternoon so I rang the hire car people up, with luck they had confirmation from the third party they had admitted liability so I received my hire car in time!

If You Ever Have A Car Accident

If you ever have the misfortune of a car accident, my advice to you is to get out the car first, then be as cool and calm as you can. As well as physical damage, mentally it can be extremely tough especially if you have a mental disability already. Running really helped me get through though, it allowed me to process how I was going to handle the challenge. My advice to you is to take up a form of running or exercise, this will give you the belief you need to beat the challenge.

I'm glad to say that nearly 10 months on I now have my car back, annoyingly I'm still having to go through my insurance to get my excess back but soon enough that will be completed. Anyway, over and out, I'm off for a run...

MY BEDROOM

Let's talk about my bedroom. This is my safe space, this is the heart of myself. It's a place I can go for escapism, and it's something that's such an important part of my life. I like to think of my bedroom as a place I can go to for safety and to escape from all the people and talking. At the minute my bedroom is a room in this psychiatric ward, it has elements of my bedroom at home, but it's not my bedroom. Being in this hospital, I'm learning to use it as my safe space though, I'm thinking of it as a place I can go to for comfort and safety when things get a bit too much. I just lie down and forget about everything and I'm going to reiterate this to my nurses from now on, it's important I tell them that my safe space is my room, so if I need to go for lie down, I go, and I'm sure they'll take me. I even brought a big white teddy into my room to make me feel more safe, I'm not afraid to say I cuddle it at night.

"This is my safe space, this is the heart of me, my bedroom."

Now let's talk about my real bedroom, the one at home. My room is so creative, I've made it all Harry Potter themed so everywhere you look there's something from the boy wizard. As you walk in there's a sign that says "Wizards Welcome, Muggles Tolerated", so if any Muggle stops by, they are fully aware. If you're not tuned up to Harry Potter, a wizard is a wizard, I'm pretty sure you know what that is, a muggle is a person of non-magical powers so a person like you and I. I've got a long list of Harry Potter characters as you walk in alongside other famous Harry Potter quotes including "Always" by Severus Snape and "I Solemnly Swear That I am Up To No Good" as well as a picture of the Hogwarts crest. I've also kitted out my bedroom with all sorts of Harry Potter models, I've collected over 20 Harry Potter Pop Funko figures which really makes the room feel all HP, that's Harry Potter not the sauce.

You see, I live in a council house with my Mum. Before we moved in, I made sure it was painted white and then I bought black vinyl stickers with Harry Potter quotes and stuck them up as well as pictures of the Hogwarts crest and a list of character names from the Harry Potter movies. This is my creative side coming through, I love designing things and being in this mental health hospital that's shown through too. I love colouring in, painting and doing artwork, at the minute I'm struggling with concentration but I need to say when things are getting a bit too much, which I am as I'm becoming more confident each and every day I'm in here.

"I solemnly swear that I am up to no good."

Harry Potter is plastered all over my bedroom but you know what else is, running. My bedroom is where I created my runningwithdan.com blog which of course is now livingwithda.com. I have my medals hung up in my bedroom, most of them are on the end of a curtain pole. I really must spread them out a bit more they are my biggest achievement to date. Actually, a lot of my medals are at my Dads at the minute but I'm sure they're being kept safe for me.

See, when I got taken into this mental health hospital I had two or three different bedrooms, I had no structure, things were going all over the place which led me to destruction. Not having a safe space meant I didn't sleep for weeks on end which ultimately led to more and more stress on my brain. This is why it's so important to have this safe space, a place where I can go to re-group after concentrating for so long. If I don't have the security of a safe zone I start to panic.

"My safe space is where I created running with dan."

Today, I met with my Mum and see showed me my new bedroom for when I get home, out of this mental health hospital. My Mum and my sister have spent hours doing it up, they binned all the old bills I had from a while ago and tidied everything in my room. They showed me pictures of it and my new safe space looks amazing, I can't wait to get their but I know it's slow stages, I know it will be more than likely two weeks until I leave, I just need to pace myself. Part of me is a bit worried about going home and living in a newly decorated safe space, for example I'm worried about finding my things but I know deep down, once I get used to everything, it will all be fine.

When I got ill I turned my safe space into what I called a palace of positivity, I stuck all sorts of positive quotes from my Instagram all over the walls to make it a feel like a good environment. There was all sorts of positive quotes stuck on my wall, ones like "anything is possible", "life is for living, grab it with both hands.", "26.2 miles, that's not far". I love these positive quotes, ask any runner they'll agree with me, a positive mind means a positive body which means a positive person.

That's why I stuck the positive quotes all over my wall because I knew it would make me more positive, unfortunately it made me slightly too positive and this positive mindset overtook my mind.

BLOG EXTRACT: HOW I STARTED RUNNING

Let me take you back to October 2017, as you may have read I was sat in a Bingo Hall, severely overweight, feeling very anxious, needing something to break free from. Then I signed up to Portsmouth's Great South Run and my life changed dramatically.

So, how can I start?

To begin with, there's something I'd like you to consider, what if you were taken hostage, forced on a treadmill on the highest setting and forced to run for at least 2 hours whilst being fed continuous doses of sugar and water. What would happen? Would you survive? Would you even make it out alive? OF COURSE YOU WOULD!

"It's All In The Mind."

The point I'm trying to get across to you is that running is ALL IN THE MIND. It's YOU that makes that decision to put on those trainers, it's YOU that makes that decision to go outside on a cold frosty morning, it's YOU that runs a marathon because you've been training continuously for the past year, it's YOU. In other words, if you want to lose weight and start running, go and run.

How far should I run?

To begin with I recommend running at least 2-3 times a week. There's no need for any gym sessions yet as you need to get used to running on the road. The hills, the bumps, the flat, knowing how to deal with these during your running is key. When you start you'll probably begin to feel stiff after the first few runs especially if they are a longer distance, listen to your body, don't push it too hard as you may suffer an injury. Remember, the more you run, the easier it gets.

TALKING

Having Aspergers I hate talking, I hate the conversation, what's the point in talking, it's pointless, it's only useful if you want to ask someone something. I go to parties and see people talking and chatting each other up and think, "how on earth do you find the words to speak?". If you're reading this with Aspergers or autism, you're probably chuckling to yourself because you realise the same thing, the majority of the time, talking is pointless, it's not needed.

> "I go to work and see endless amounts of pointless meetings taking place."

I go to work and see endless amounts of pointless meetings taking place. I go down the town and see so many people just endlessly talking to each other about nothing. Talking wastes so much time in our daily life, we're so busy but if we take a step back surely the answer is to do less talking and focus on the task in hand. For example, I'm sat here writing this book now, I've written nearly 7,500 words but what if I started talking. I'm wasting time when I could be generating more words for this book. Talking is such a distraction in our everyday life, if we didn't have talking we'd get so much more done.

Whilst I don't enjoy talking, I also don't enjoy the noise social scenes create. The amount of times you're at a party and you hear everyone else chatting away to each other, whilst you're stood there wondering what on earth you do. That's having Aspergers, the moment you're stood around not knowing what to do whilst everyone else knows exactly how to communicate and interpret the world.

The last time I was in this situation I was at the WOBA Awards (West Oxfordshire Business Awards). I had successfully got my work to the semi-finals of the local business awards and I had to go as I was the organiser. I arrived half an hour early and was waiting for my colleagues who hadn't tuned up. I had been waiting 15 minutes in the car so then I decided to go in, well go and stand by the entrance for another 15 minutes, I got a bit cold but I said myself that's okay, I waited another 15 minutes and the event started so I had to go in and ask for a name badge and go and stand in the hall, not knowing any of these companies whilst I waited for my colleagues who turned up 30 minutes late. This was terrifying but I did it, see this is how much my confidence has grown since back when I was a child.

"What's the point in the conversation?"

I tend to only talk if I need to talk, so if I need more loo roll, I'll ask for some. That's an example of talk I've been using in this mental health hospital. So, for example, I'd process the speech as "can I have more toilet roll?" and the reply is "Yes, I'll get you some.", but then there's a multitude of other things that could happen within the conversation. Plus, with the amount of Doctors and Nurses in this hospital, a multitude of things could happen. This is where we as people with Aspergers struggle because we can only process one thought at a time, so every conversation we have, has to be planned and go in a certain direction. So that toilet roll needs to be in my hands almost immediately after I've asked for it, if not I'm going to start panicking. Imagine every conversation you have needing to be planned like this? This is what life is like with Aspergers.

Processing conversational thought is so difficult for me and for many people diagnosed with the condition. One thing that has really helped me though is my running.

Running has transformed the way I live, I feel so much more confident, it's like I'm a different person. I can process thought slightly easier through running, as running releases that "feel good" endorphin into my system. Running has made me a new person, just read my blog "How Running Changed My Life" and that will tell you how much of a person I've become. I get up early, I eat healthy, I sleep straight through, that's how much running changed me. Unfortunately the stress of running and doing a bit too much plus coronavirus led me here. It's led me to be in this mental health hospital.

See if you have Aspergers you try to achieve things no matter how hard they may seem, so if I want to be the best runner on the planet, I'll do it, no matter how hard it may seem, if I want to write this book, I'll do it, no matter how difficult it may seem. The thing is my brain is recovering from a psychotic episode so I can't push myself too much. That's why I'm carefully writing this book and relaxing in-between stages of writing it. If it starts to get too much I'll stop immediately, pack up and go to sleep.

BLOG EXTRACT: READY TO RUN SILVERSTONE

Tomorrow I take on one of the flattest races I could ever run, Run Silverstone. If you're not aware, that's the UK most popular Formula One track so it's meant to very flat. Now a month or so ago I was on a cruise around Europe.

I was eating breakfast, lunch, afternoon tea, dinner and then late snacks. After some pretty hard training I think I'm ready to run. I'm hoping I can run anything under my PB (1 hour, 37 minutes, 54 seconds), breaking an hour and a half would be incredible but I think I need to do a bit more training until that happens. Five or so years ago, I took on this race and finished in 2 hours 10 minutes, so it's incredible how far I've come since then.

Anyway, I hope you're enjoying reading my brand new website. Don't forget you can follow me on Twitter, Facebook and Instagram. I'll be updating you on my progress as I run around Silverstone and of course, showing of my medal and merchandise I receive when I cross the finish line!

MUSIC

When it comes to music our family is full of playful hits. I remember the classic song my Mum used to sing at the table every time we eat Jelly:

"Jelly, jelly, wobbly and cold,
Jelly, jelly in a bowl.
Dip the spoon in, one, two, three,
Here's some jelly just for me."

Bedtime was one special time when we were younger too, I remember my Mum and Dad singing special songs such as the notable hit:

"I'm a big fat bin, round and fat
Bend me in now I'm flat.
Now it's time to go to bed,
So go to sleep,
Non night."

Then there was the huge hit:

"See you in the morning
See you in the evening.
See you when you get up,
Non night."

To anyone reading this you might think my family's mad, after all according to the sign hung up on our front door, as far as anyone knows "we're a nice, normal family" and we are, we just like singing songs to each other about jelly and broken bins before we go to bed.

"Jelly and bins featured heavily on the night time playlist."

To tell you the truth, it was my brother who broke the bin, he stepped on it before he was going to bed, that's why we sing about a broken bin before we go to bed.

ORGANISATION

When it comes to organisation, I'm extremely organised. If you had to score my organisation out of 100 I'd say I was more than 100. Having Aspergers as well as OCD makes me super, super organised as I know exactly what I'm going to do on a day to day basis.

"I really couldn't be any more organised."

For example, I woke up this morning inside this mental health hospital, well the place I call home for now on, I've had Breakfast, I've had a shower and I am know writing this book until 11am. At 11am I'm going to watch a little bit of TV to relax before my lunch at 12pm. After lunch at 12pm, I'm going to have a sleep before I have the gym at 2pm. After 2pm, I'm meeting my Dad and my sister outside for an hour before I'm going to learn how to draw at 4pm. Then I have dinner at 5pm where I'll go and watch TV on my laptop or in the TV lounge before I go to sleep at 8.30pm. That's my day, it's a really, really long day but I get through it, I know I'll get through it, it's just pure organisation. If you still don't believe me here's an example of one my days:

9am – My alarm's already set from the night before so it's time to get up, have a shower and get going. First thing's first though, I have to make my bed, of course I need to leave a tidy room, then once my bed's been made, head to the bathroom to have a shave, shower and if needed s**t.

10am – I should have had a shower by now, if I don't have a shower before 10am I kind of start freaking out unless there is a completely valid reason, like I've been for a run. In that case, the shower should be free for me to jump into when I get home. The amount of times I've come back home and the shower is in use. I need to try and calm myself in situations like this though, I just need to say to myself, it's okay if someone is in the shower, I can wait. Anyway, if I haven't been for a run, I usually go for a walk with my Mum at 10am.

11am – After getting back from my walk, this hour requires me to do something small. I only have an hour until lunch so it doesn't have to be too strenuous, keep it small and simple.

1pm – Lunch done, now we are in to the afternoon. That means I need to focus on several bigger projects like writing my book for example. After writing my book I can do things like play on my PS4 or Nintendo Switch or do some art.

2pm – Still writing my book, if I start to struggle, I'll go for a lie down.

3pm – Think it's time for a little lie down. I like listening to podcasts whilst I'm relaxing and having a chill out, that's what me and my Mum are calling it.

4pm – Time for a little bit of EastEnders. A little bit of TV in the afternoon is good for keeping me relaxed.

5pm – Getting towards tea time now, so it's best to ask Mum what's for tea.

6pm – Tea time should be now, if it's any later I do get a bit panicky. I need to learn to relax and if we have it slightly later it doesn't matter at all.

7pm – Tea time could be now, if it's earlier or later, I can think of other things I can do during that time.

8pm – Going for a walk with my Mum, evening walks are good for winding down.

9pm – I'm going to bed, must remember to have had my medication before falling asleep though.

10pm – I'll be fast asleep by 10pm ready to do it all again the next day.

I wish we all could be as organised as me, the amount of people I see walking down the street not knowing where they are going, having pointless meetings, wasting minutes just simply talking. That's why an Asperger's brain is so much more powerful than a normal brain (not to be biased) because I am always on the go and have a structure I need to follow. The things is, when that structure changes, the whole world changes, hence why I'm here in this mental health hospital. For example, in this hospital this morning I wanted to have a shave but it had run out of battery life, so I started panicking and messaged my Dad to say can he bring me up a wet razor and shaving foam. He is visiting me this afternoon so it's okay but at the end of the day if I don't have a shave, it's not the end of the world, I'm still alive on the planet, I'm still here and I exist and that's the most important thing.

"I wish we all could be as organised as me."

Organisation isn't just the result of my Aspergers, it's the result of having OCD too. I like certain things to be in place at a certain time, if that changes, everything changes. I have many common OCD traits, I'll check the light switch to see if it's off, I'll check my phone to see how much battery is left, I'll check the car door to see whether it's locked. These habits are just a form of security for me, I like things to be a certain way and in a certain place. For example, I like my phone to be by my bed, I like my bed to be made as soon as I get up, I like certain items to be here and there. In my bedroom, I'll have my keys, phone and wallet lined up in a box formation.

BLOG EXTRACT: HOW RUNNING CHANGED MY LIFE

If you didn't know, I have Aspergers Syndrome, to put it simply, Aspergers means I struggle in social situations and I struggle with confidence. Running however has changed that completely, it's changed my life.

Confidence

Just 10 years ago I used to be afraid just to walk into a shop and buy something. I remember my Mum saying to me as we approached a shop "You going to go in and have a look then?". I hesitatingly refused and she had to come in with me.

Since I've been running, I'm a different person. Last February, before I ran the London Marathon I organised my own charity raffle for Sobell House. I had to walk into local shops and businesses and ask, YES ASK THEM WITH MY OWN MOUTH, if they'd like to offer me a prize or buy a ticket for my raffle. I thoroughly believe this would not have been possible without running being part of my life. The raffle raised an incredible £2,000 for charity by the way! Other examples of my confidence coming through include organising a boat party with my work, whilst I'm able to hold a conversation much better too. Yes, I still struggle at times due to my Aspergers but I feel much more confident.

Diet

Believe it or not, I actually love eating fruit, vegetables and salad. I'm eating stuff I would have never have eaten when I was overweight. I'd much prefer to have a roast, than a burger. The healthier I become, the more healthier I'd rather eat.

Sleep

Right, any runner would agree with me, the best time to run is 6.30am on a well, sunny (if possible) day as the sun's rising. You may be reading this as a non-runner thinking "Are you nuts?". Well, I can tell you now, I'm not. In fact, I can't sleep much longer than 6.30am. If I go to bed at 10-10.30pm, I'm up at 6am onwards. When I say I'm up, I mean I'm ready to go, motivated, feeling like I'm on top of the world. I'm not tired, depressed, feeling awful, needing a coffee to get me going in the morning.

The Way I See The World

"We all go to work 9-5pm, sit in traffic, eat takeaways, get obese and then we die. "

Lastly, running's made me see the world in a new way. For example, having Aspergers, I pay a lot of attention to detail, so as I run I often hear the birds chirping and the wind rushing through my hair. I've also noticed how more and more people are suffering from anxiety and depression. We all go to work 9-5pm, sit in traffic, eat takeaways, get obese and then we die. If we take a look back at what I've written, isn't running or exercise for that matter the answer to living a happier and healthier life, quite clearly it is.

ASTHMA

One thing I haven't mentioned in my book is my Asthma. When I was younger I nearly died of an Asthma attack, according to my Mum my oxygen level was at 76%. That was really low and I was severely struggling to breath, but I hung on and survived the attack because I'm a fighter, I don't give in.

Even as I'm sat here now, writing this in hospital, I'm struggling to write this book, I just want to go back to bed but I know I need to be out and about, tackling new challenges rather than just staying in a hospital bed. This is exactly what Ant Middleton talks about in his book "The Fear Bubble". Ant Middleton goes on to talk about how we're living in a protected society, how we're constantly being told not to do stuff and stay protected rather than taking on new challenges. Taking on new challenges is why I've been so successful, why I've got a degree, why I've become a confident person because I'm always up for a challenge and facing death by being told you've got 76% of oxygen in your body is a fantastic example of how I'm fighter and I never give in, despite how hard the challenge maybe.

"I'm a fighter, I don't give in."

Asthma plays a huge part in my life and it certainly has changed the lives of my peers around me. I don't suffer with Asthma anymore but my brothers suffer terribly with it, they have been in and out of hospital more times than a TV boxset of Casualty and Holby City put together. I can't count the number of times I've been home and they have been sent up to hospital with breathing difficulties. I'm glad to say they are okay now and they are also getting through the worst.

Some of the language I've been using can come across a bit selfish. That's the thing with Aspergers it can make you seem selfish. For example, in the previous paragraph I've made a joke about the amount of times my brothers have been in and out of hospital. The problem is that my mind is taking that "selfish" approach as I know that my brothers going into hospital has caused me a collapse of structure which I go on and on about, time and time again. Structure is key to people with Aspergers. my brother's trips to hospital meant I didn't go on holiday one year which meant I didn't go away. It's not that I'm being selfish it's just that it caused me so much strain and change of structure I remember their time in hospital in a negative light.

TECHNOLOGY

If anything technology seems to make my OCD worse, I'm continually checking for chargers and whether my phone has enough battery life. In this mental health hospital, I'm always trying to keep phone topped up with battery life and I'm always worrying it will run out.

"Technology and me sort of get on."

The thing is I need my phone as it's a sense of security for me but I don't need to keep worrying about it. If it does run out of battery, I can always contact my Sister or Brother using a different method such as my laptop or the office phone. I must also tell myself that my Mum isn't simply going to leave me in this mental health hospital, they are fully supportive of me, I can get out as soon as I'm better. Also, I can use the main phone line if I desperately want to talk to someone. I know my Mum's coming today too which is good as I know she will be here at around 3pm. I've got dinner, then a nice sleep, then the gym before a bit more of my book then I have the evening. The thing is being in this mental health hospital when you're struggling to focus, it can get hard and can get boring at times. The good news is my focus seems to be improving in here the more sleep I'm getting the better I am at focusing.

TRANSPORT

If someone gave me a choice between driving a car, cycling or walking, I'd probably choose walking. Walking is so less stressful than getting in to a car and driving it. To tell you the truth, I'm enjoying having time off driving right now, I don't miss it one bit whilst I'm recovering from my psychotic episode. The majority of the time there's so many cars on the road it would be quicker walking. That's why I'd choose to walk if I had the option, obviously if it's quite a distance, I'd choose to cycle as that's exercise as well.

"Traffic would be in my room 101."

What really annoys me is the amount of people I see simply sat in their cars, with their engine running just chilling; it's so annoying seeing people just sat there, killing the environment with their engines blasting out fumes. It's like they're saying to themselves "I'm just going to sit here, watch the world go by and let my engine pump out as many fumes as it can". I mean, it's ridiculous, why not go to your destination, drive from A to B, get out the car and go into the shop or place you were going too, don't just sit in the car and wait, unless it's a job interview that is.

"So many things could go wrong whilst driving."

I mean the only time I've ever sat in a car for a long period of time is before a job interview or if I'm waiting to go into a social event. I don't regularly pitch up by a kerb, leave my lights on, radio blaring and stare at my phone, I wouldn't dream of doing that, the battery might fail. See, there's so many things that could go wrong in a car, that's why I hate driving them, you get a puncture, you get a flat battery, a bulb go out, you can't start it, the list is endless. That's why I'm kind of glad I'm not driving for now. I know that when I need to drive I'll be ready, I mean I spent 3 years without driving back when I was at University and still went on to drive.

I mean the stress you get when trying to park a car too, I mean have you seen the amount of spaces there are in town, there's none, none whatsoever, unless you are a master at parking and can park a car in the gap the size of a snail. I mean this is exactly what driving causes me, stress. I really think driving's played a huge part in the reason I got ill, there's so much stress and I was driving more than 300 miles a week. The good news is that I won't have to drive so much when I get out of this mental health hospital as I'll have to refer myself to the DVLA for an assessment. I will have a bus pass I can use though to go into town whenever I want to.

One good thing coronavirus has done is ease the pollution in the world, there has been a whole load of cars removed from society, for a temporary period of course. I think this will really help save the planet in the long run as many cars have been removed from their daily commute.

BLOG EXTRACT: THE NATIONAL RUNNING SHOW #BESTDAYEVER

I've just got back from the National Running Show at Birmingham's NEC. It was amazing, if you're a runner I really recommend it next year. The talks, the stands and most importantly, the FREEBIES! I got free porridge, a t-shirt, a copy of Runners World, a ton of NUUN energy drink and a goody bag filled with goodies courtesy of Runderwear!

Belief

To be honest when I first arrived at the show I wasn't sure if it would be any good, I knew I had to approach stands and talk to people, not good if you have Aspergers but with a little confidence, I did it more and more. I come across Steve Cram talking about belief, everything he said was exactly how I would have worded it, you see everyone passing their driving test and they succeed so you expect to succeed so why don't you feel the same with running, you see an elite runner and think that's impossible but if you believe, anything is possible just as I believe.

Connection

It was amazing to meet @TheRealMelHeale, to be able to meet a Twitter friend and bring my community to the real world was incredible. I realised how similar we are as runners, before arriving at the show I noticed how many people were choosing to take the steps instead of the moving platform or elevators. It's our way of thinking, I just love it. I listened to an amazing talk from Jessica Robson from @runtalkrun who had the guts to go on stage and talk about her experience suffering with bulimia and depression. I'm hoping to launch my own Run Talk Run group in the future, look out for it!

Running Is Not A Solo Sport

Lastly, running is definitely not a solo sport. We're a community and it's a community I want to keep on growing, together us runners, we'll change the world! 👍🏃♂

FUNDRAISING

Running has really made me more confident. In fact, it's turned me into a completely new person, I'm so much more confident talking around other people. I'm not saying it gets any easier, I have to push myself quite a bit to create conversation but I'm such a more confident person. Back in 2019, I organised my own charity Easter raffle for my London Marathon fundraising. I raised just under £2,000 which was an incredible achievement for me. I had to gather the prizes and email a whole load of companies asking for prizes, I received prize after prize, a local Indian Takeaway kindly offered me a £10 voucher, Oxford Playhouse generously donated two tickets to a show of choice, a local hairdresser offered me a prize, Blenheim Palace donated a family ticket, plus the local Transport Museum offered me a family ticket too.

"My Easter raffle was a huge achievement."

Once I had gathered all of the prizes, I had to sell the tickets. I designed them using a raffle ticket creator I found online. They looked really good and had a picture of me wearing my Sobell House running t-shirt on them. Selling the raffle tickets was a difficult task for me, I remember stopping off at a pub on the way to work and asking if they wanted to buy any of my tickets, I went down to Eynsham Hall and asked the people there if they wanted to buy any, I went to my local dentist and they bought some too. I literally went into any place you can think of and asked if they wanted to buy some tickets. I drew the raffle live on my Facebook profile so everyone could see if they had won a prize. My Sister's boyfriend, Jack won a lot of the prizes, my boss at work won a couple of them too whilst some also went to my Nan's friends and family. Ultimately, the raffle was a huge success and raised over £2,000 for Sobell House.

"My next fundraising challenge will be for MIND."

Fundraising takes a lot a time and it's something I want to continue but this time for the charity, MIND. MIND are going to be one of my dedicated charities from now on simply because they mean a lot and I know how difficult using your MIND can be. My Mum goes and visits the local MIND charities regularly, every Thursday she goes down to them and they help her focus and live with her anxiety. My Mum isn't the only one who struggles with her anxiety, my sister and brothers both do and so do I.

In fact, as part of my fundraising I'm thinking of putting on a talk at the charity MIND with them about my life, about how I've overcome my mental health and have written this book, which is going to be a book when I've found the 50,000 words. The presentation will be about me but will also encourage the people at MIND to donate or come up with ways we can raise funds for MIND. I might even start creating a presentation and practising it now whilst I'm here in this mental health hospital and I have the time. I feel a presentation will really encourage those who go to MIND to find ways to fundraise.

In fact, we've already started fundraising, my family raised £100 for MIND this May by organising a charity race night, I hope to keep the fundraising coming, especially for MIND. MIND are going to be one of my dedicated charities from now on simply because they mean a lot and I know how difficult using your MIND can be. I'm also planning on fundraising for the New York Marathon soon.

"What makes people donate?"

The question you have to ask yourself is what makes people donate to a charity? People have to connect and if people don't connect then people won't give. See with fundraising you're continually trying to give people a reason to donate. The truth is a lot of people are selfish they don't like giving; the charity has to really connect with them for them to give. That's why my fundraising will connect with them as I will share my story far and wide. I will share it through a presentation at the charity MIND, on social media when I'm ready and everywhere I can think off. I might even make a short film about my story and play it to them. If I can really get people connected with my story they will donate.

That's not all I just spoke to one of the nurses at this mental health hospital, his name was Austin and he is going to make me a role model for people with mental health difficulties in Africa. That means this book will connect with thousands of people in Africa. See, I'm a role model to those people in Africa because I have shown them that there is life after having extreme mental difficulties, there is life if you have a form of autism or Aspergers. I simply believed there was a way and I'm slowly recovering.

"I hope this book and my story goes far and wide."

I'm also proposing that 50% of the profits made from this book will go to the charity MIND, that's one way to boost my fundraising. By sharing my story I'm reconnecting with those with mental health difficulties, giving them a reason to buy this book which ultimately will raise millions for the mental health charity, MIND. That's the connection that will help my fundraising, that's the connection I am after, the personal connection. Thousands of people have mental health difficulties, I have one personal story and I'm willing to share it with you in this book.

BLOG EXTRACT: THE REAL REASON I RUN

Imagine being 18 stone? Walking around feeling like you're carrying two of you? Feeling like you're being drowned in fat, unable to breath, every step you take feels like extra, phenomenal effort.

It's horrible, disgusting and something I never want to go back too. Some people say food is like a drug, we eat too much and we always feel horrible after. But what made me choose to change my life? Why did I wake up one day and say, you know what Dan I'm going to start running?

"I remember that feeling, being free, being able to breath easily, feeling confident, feeling like you're on top of the world"

I had lost weight and ran a half marathon in 2010 but I had put all this weight back on again. I remembered the time when I had lost weight in 2010, I remembered that feeling, being free, being able to breathe easily, feeling confident, feeling like you're on top of the world, feeling like you can do anything. I'm pleased to say this has come across in my job as well as my life. I knew taking up running wasn't impossible. I took these thoughts and stepped out the door. I knew I had to do something that would change my life forever.

If you want to start running and lose weight, it's not impossible. Start by signing up to a challenge, let's say a 10k or a virtual run, allow plenty of time to train. If you sign up to a challenge, you'll have no choice but to train and you'll soon never want to stop. As I've said before, running is a drug, once you start you'll never want to stop.

DRAMA

Moving further back in my life, what has really helped me with my confidence, is my passion for Drama. Drama allows me to become a different person. I always think to myself, "if this was a play, how would I act?" and apply that to real world situations. I used to belong to a Drama group where I played several big parts; the only thing I couldn't do though and still wish to this day I could, is sing. I had to play the parts which didn't involve singing which in musicals, there aren't many. Luckily, I played several huge parts that don't sing such as I played the Wizard in the Wizard Of Oz and Henry Miller in Calamity Jane. I stopped Drama because I started getting the fear that I would forget my words, maybe this was anxiety and I didn't know about it, thinking back. I enjoyed Drama and I kind of want to start at it again in the future.

"The one thing I wish I could do is sing."

In terms of Drama, I'm not scared to go on the actual stage, if anything I love going on stage and acting. I was watching a TED Talk a month or so ago, it was by Jordan

Raskopoulos, she spoke about living with High Functioning Anxiety, which is the same as High Functioning Autism, I'm no Doctor but I've just Googled it and a lot of therapist say it's the same thing. Anyway, in her TED talk, Raskopoulos was talking about how she isn't scared to go stage, which I'm not, she knows how to speak on stage, which I do, she knows how to communicate, which I do. What she doesn't know how to do though is communicate in social situations, she's more nervous in social situations, which is exactly the same as I feel. I love the stage, I love being on it if I don't have certain words I need to say, I love presenting to people and giving them something to love.

In terms of stage shows, I've been to many in the West End. I have program after program I've collected from stage shows and football matches across the country. I've seen many good shows, I remember going to see the Lion King at school, *SPOILER ALERT* a giant elephant starts coming down the aisle at the start of the show and there are animals, well humans that look like animals that jump around all over the place. I remember Simba and Nana, I think that's what they're called, start riding giant emu's whilst singing "I Just Can't Wait To Be King". Chitty Chitty Bang Bang was really good to, I remember seeing the flying car, in fact it was revolutionary for the time and broke records at the

London Palladium. I've been to the London Palladium twice, once to see Chitty Chitty Bang Bang and the other to see the Sound Of Music with my Nan and Aunty.

"Drama allows me to be someone else on stage."

I love songs from the musicals too, watching them is amazing but listening to songs from the musicals really cheers me up. My favourite musical score has to be Les Miserables, I just love the songs in it, in fact I was going to be in it with my Drama group but I think the pressure got too much for me. I was in the middle of my exams at the time and didn't have any help, I literally remembered my whole syllabus at school and I think memorising that along with my Drama was too much for me to handle, so I left just before I turned 18.

I still have a passion for Drama though; I try and go to the theatre as much as I can. I get really frustrated when I see the prices of theatre tickets, some tickets are priced over £100, that's really extortionate and some people can't afford that kind of money. I noticed the Blackpool Grand Theatre were offering tickets at no more than £20 each for under 25s which I thought was a terrific idea as not many youngsters like the theatre, they prefer the cinema. I went to see Ken Dodd at the Blackpool Grand Theatre, it was a long night, I ended up leaving at 11pm and he still hadn't finished his show, rumours had it that it ended at 1am, I would have been fast asleep if I had stopped until then. Ken Dodd was known for that, his shows went on for hours which I find fascinating.

FINDING LOVE

Finding love is something so, so difficult for me. It's a bit of an embarrassing area but I've got to address it. How do I find love? How does someone with Aspergers find love? I mean there are so many obstacles that you need to overcome in order to find love, I mean finding a friend is hard enough. To put things in perspective, I'm 30 and I've never been in a relationship. I mean, I've been quite close to girls in the past but in a professional manner, I was friends with a girl called Jackie whilst I was at University, she was really friendly and I really got on with her but because of her culture and ethics she wouldn't have been right as my girlfriend.

There's so many questions that need asking when it comes to finding love, like "What do you say?", "Do you share a bed?", "When do you kiss?". So how do we combat these difficulties, first I need to find someone willing to love me, like I love them. But how do I do it, how do I find love when I don't socialise? Plus all of the dating sites cost a small fortune.

How on earth do you find a "girl" friend?

I've thought about dating sites but they are so difficult to get a reply, you post a trustworthy message and then get no response. I'm going to be open and honest, I've used POF (Plenty Of Fish), Match.com and an app called Nearby. I'm not going to pay to communicate with others though, why should I pay to be able to send a message to someone, you can do that for free anyway on other sites such as Facebook or Twitter. Now I'm thinking this book could help me out on the dating scene as it literally is my life story. I remember that TV program called "This Is Your Life" where a presenter came out, I can't remember his name but he started looking back over their life with a red book. This is kind of like that, except I'm writing the book.

What do you say?

When you finally meet someone you're not instantly their girlfriend, what do you say to them to make them feel loved? That's another huge question to dissect. It's hard enough processing a conversation, let alone trying to chat them up, whatever "chatting up" is. I guess when you meet someone you just talk about what you like, if not silence is just as good. This comes back to "the art of conversation", it's so difficult for me to process conversation so I think if I were to get a girlfriend I need to let her know I have Aspergers, I need to let her know this instantly, then she can become aware of how I talk, well I talk when there's a need to talk as I explain in the previous chapter.

How do you share a bed?

How can anyone share a bed with someone, it must be so uncomfortable sharing a bed. I mean I'll be constantly pulling the duvet over me. When I sleep I like the duvet to be tucked all over me, so I'm tucked right in, that's my kind of comfortable night's sleep. If I had a girlfriend we'd need a king size duvet and bed, that way I would feel more comfortable, I suppose I'd get used to it in the end.

When do you have sex?

This is a very embarrassing subject especially to write in my book but it's something that needs addressing, after all I'm going to be open and honest. I mean I know the way sex is represented in adult movies is a completely false representation, that's me subtlety admitting to watching them by the way. Anyway, I guess it's at night time, but I know that's something that comes later into the relationship.

Do you share?

One thing I don't like doing is sharing. In a relationship I guess it's pretty much all sharing stuff, like sharing presents at Christmas. It's not that I'm selfish it's just that I like my own stuff, I like my stuff being a certain way, I like my stuff to be mine, that's my OCD. Plus in the bedroom, I can't let her near my things, they are my things, no one touches my stuff. See, this is what I mean by "sharing", my Aspergers and OCD makes it hard for me to accept having to share my stuff.

Do I buy her presents?

If I had a girlfriend I wouldn't want to buy her presents. Some people think I'm tight with money but I'm not it's just me being careful as having Aspergers I also look to the worst possible situation. For example, if I lost my job I would have no money, no money means no house which means sleeping on the streets, which means smelling, having dirty clothes and then dying. That's the worst possible scenario and that's what I'm always worrying about as I write this book, having no money. So going back to the idea of me buying my girlfriend a present, it's not that I'm tight to buy her one, it's the fear of losing everything, but of course I would buy her presents on an occasional basis.

Once I'm out of this mental health hospital, my sister has said she will help me find a relationship and show me properly how to use them. I'm sure there's someone out there to take care of me and look after me and likewise, me look after them.

One thing that will help me trigger love is my need for relaxation in my life, I've never really relaxed, I'm always a person to get up of the sofa and be on the get go, that's why I'm a runner of course. I think I need to make time and just chill from now on, it's okay to just sit down and do nothing, not think and just have relaxation time. If anything it's good to have this time as I can have creative space, a chance to go over any creative ideas and come up with new ones. I'm such a creative person, if anything; this relaxation time will help me come up with even greater creative ideas in the future.

WEATHER

Snow, rain, wind or sun, I'll be outside whatever the weather. As a runner I'll run in anything, this is one trait of my Aspergers, weather or circumstance doesn't bother you and weather is certainly one of them. You'll face the harsh conditions even if it means slipping over on ice. In fact I nearly did once, I was on a run coming back from Brackley and I nearly slipped over on pure ice going downhill, a car was coming towards me and I completely lost control. I could have seriously hurt myself that day but I didn't, I survived and I was okay.

> "Rain or snow, the weather doesn't bother me."

Accepting circumstance is what makes me such a loving and caring person, it's the attitude we all should take. If something cannot happen it doesn't matter, you just have to try it again another day.

I always tend to make silly decisions too, for example if the shower has no hot water I'll still use it even though it's cold. It's what makes me such a kind and loving person, if someone can't do something I'll say "that's okay" and accept it and just move on rather than face reality. That's why I can run in any weather condition, except snow of course because snow can get really slippy and it's hard to grip your feet on the road.

TELEVISION

I've never actually been much of a fan of watching television. Back whilst I was at University I did some work looking into the construction of the house, why do most living rooms have a TV at the centre of it? It's an interesting question and it's something I want to explore aside from this book. Why do we enter a house and the first thing that's at the centre of it is a TV box? It really frustrates me, I often blank the TV because I don't want constructed messages by the media being thrown towards me, why do I have to put the TV on and face a bombardment of media messages. I mean, why can't a bookcase be at the centre of the living room or an object people can admire, not a box with a multitude of message built in it.

If you think about it, we're told to live a certain way of life, we're told we should have breakfast, have lunch, have dinner. What if we're told something different, what if suddenly it became bad for you to eat 3 meals a day, what would we do then? See what I'm saying is, having Aspergers I notice a lot of attention to detail, I realise the media are creating messages within society and we follow them, I realise the TV is pumping out messages the media want us to act upon or in other words, turn the TV on.

"TV isn't my cup of tea at the minute."

I can't count the amount of times I've walked into a living room and blanked the TV, well that is until my Dad comes in and says *"put the TV on if you want to Dan"*. That said, I often tend to listen to my Dad and put the TV on, hoping something good is about to come on. In terms of TV when I was younger, the show I loved the most was Chucklevision, I just found it hilarious, two old men trying to do DIY. My Mum recorded most of the episodes on the old VHS, boy I remember VHS. It's amazing to think how you can now simply press a button to record something whereas years ago you had to collect piles and piles of VHS tapes.

Another one of my favourite children TV shows has to be a show I used to watch called Bernard's Watch. It first aired on the 8th September 1995 and ended production on the 31st March 2005. You've probably figured out the show's format, it was about a boy named Bernard who had a watch, it was his watch hence the name Bernard's Watch. This watch was no ordinary watch it could STOP time, when I say STOP time, I mean literally STOP everything. I used to imagine the things I could do if I had this watch, it would be incredible to just simply STOP everything, Arnie the local Ice Cream Man, Jennie shopping in Superdrug and Brian the Butcher, they would all have to halt their day because you simply pressed STOP. You wouldn't have to pay for anything either because you could walk into a shop press STOP and walk out, go home and then press START again. That's probably why I enjoyed the show so much, thinking of all the things you could do if you stopped time when you wanted to, it was enjoyable and sparked by imagination.

"My imagination is wild like a child."

One thing I am good at is using my imagination. There are so many TV shows I loved watching when I was younger that used my imagination, Bernards Watch was just one, others included the BBC Drama The Queens Nose. This involved a young girl who finds a 50p, when she rubs the 50p her wishes come true. Again you see, another program that's using your imagination. Another BBC hit The Demon Headmaster, this was about a headmaster who was evil and I can't really remember much after that. Moving on to ITV, I loved Jungle Run, this was a quiz show format and involved several contestants running around a jungle looking for golden monkeys. Then there was 50:50, this was a quiz show too but it was between two schools. 50 people from each school went up against each other in a quiz show format. I could go on and on listing all the top quality children's TV shows I watched when I was younger. I'm thinking to myself now, why don't I go back and watch all of these again, they were so good and amazing to watch. I think every child's TV show maker should take note on my taste of TV show.

MARATHONS

I would have never thought I'd be able to run a marathon a year ago, let alone two. London and Bournemouth Marathons are the only two marathons I've run, and I'm so amazed at completing them. Running a marathon is really tough, I mean like really tough, it's such a mental challenge, especially the last 6 miles. If I had to think of things to compare the last 6 miles of a marathon too, I'd say going to a toilet with constipation or climbing Mount Everest.

"There's nothing tougher than running a marathon."

I was super confident but nervous at the same time when I ran the London Marathon. To get to the start of the London Marathon you have to climb a huge hill, that's before you even begin running. I managed to climb it though, taking it steady knowing I had 26.2 miles to cover. After climbing a huge hill I finally arrived at the Red Zone, the start of the London Marathon. Now, killing an hour and half before you have to run 26.2 miles is really, really difficult. I decided to try and kill time by trying to get on TV as I could see where they were filming. I remember walking behind the interviewees to see if I could make it, unfortunately I wasn't in the right area so I didn't get on TV.

Anyway, after killing an hour and a half I was finally on the start line, I had stretched and I was waiting behind a giant cardboard cut-out of the Queen. I mean of all the places to be before I ran the furthest distance of my life, I was behind a huge cut out of the Queen, it's better than the giant Dinosaur that was a few metres up from me. To begin with, the race was crammed with people, it felt like I was going to trip over everyone and it really wasn't nice although the crowd and the atmosphere was incredible. I've got a picture of me running past the Cutty Sark at mile 7 on my bedroom wall, I looked extremely confident and I'll remember that moment forever. One part of the London Marathon I'll really remember was running along the Embankment, it was the last 6 miles and my legs were in agony, I also felt like I was going to faint as I hadn't drank enough water. Eventually though, I made it to the finish in an incredible time of 3 hours 44 minutes.

"I'll always remember those last 6 miles along the Embankment."

That was my first marathon though; my second marathon was even harder, this was down in Bournemouth. Now one thing about marathon running I didn't realise was the importance of pacing yourself. In London I got away with not pacing myself as the ground was almost as flat as a pancake, Bournemouth however was another story. After mile 20 my legs got really, really tired and it felt like they were made of concrete. I remember dragging my feet on the seafront for 6 long miles before finally finishing in 4 hours 5 minutes. I'm so pleased to say I've run not one, but two marathons, like any runner though once you start running marathons you don't want to stop. It's stupid isn't it, it's like you want to be in pain running 26.2 miles.

Being in this psychiatric ward, it feels like I'm running a marathon every day, I'm constantly pushing myself to do the small things, like write this book for example, like have a shower, like watch TV, like do a crossword, literally I'm having to develop that push feeling for everything at the minute. Whilst I have to maintain that "PUSH" culture I also have to try and think about my rest and recovery, a lot of the time I feel I just want to go and sleep and relax in my room. This of course is okay and I'm constantly being aware if I overdo my book writing.

BLOG EXTRACT: WHAT IF YOU WERE TOLD "YOU CAN'T EXERCISE FOR 30 DAYS"?

"ARGHHHH", that's what would be running through my brain if I was told I couldn't exercise or run for 30 days. Most runners would agree with me, not exercising for 30 days would be awful, you'll lose your mind. Not being able to get your heart pumping, blood flowing and get rid of that excess fat you put on the other day, due to that recent trip to Ronald's McDonalds.

This morning I went for a 7 and a half mile run around my village. It was dark & cold there was driving rain, a ton of wind, enough to blow over a dozen elephants in fact and the conditions were pretty damn awful…. to a non-runner.

What's The Worst That Can Happen?

See if you're reading this as a non-runner, you're not looking at the bigger picture, yes there might be rain, wind and the dark to battle with, but once you've battled with it, how good do you feel? What's the worst that will happen too, you'll get a bit wet, it's a bit of water, it's too windy, that only makes you run even more rewarding as you've worked harder, it's cold, you'll warm up once you get going, it's dark, wear a head torch you'll see everything. Not just that, running in these conditions improves your immune system, I don't get colds as I'm breathing in cold, fresh air consistently as a run. Also, I've ran first thing in the morning, so I know that If I can deal with those conditions, I can deal with anything thrown at me throughout the day. It's this kind of feeling I'll be craving if I was told I couldn't exercise.

So, let me ask that question again, what if you were told you couldn't exercise for 30 days?

WATER

Drinking water is such a psychological thing when you run, the question to ask yourself is, do you really need it? I like to carry a bottle with me when I run as psychologically it means I am in a safe space. Sounds stupid doesn't it, having a bottle of water to keep you safe, to keep you within the knowledge that you won't dehydrate. It's like someone said to you, "Right, carry this water bottle, don't drink it until you get home, just carry it though, you might need it half way around.".

"Water Is An Illusion."

The thing is you don't need that water bottle, in fact that's a form of OCD, and millions upon millions of people go out running with the intention of drinking water they carry around with them but only end up taking about two sips. That's what I usually do as I don't tend to sweat when I run, only if I'm doing a longer distance do I tend to sweat. I tend to go out for a run overhydrated, I tell you how I know this, my urines usually white and clear that's how I know, not that you needed to know.

Carrying a water bottle is simply an illusion, sometimes it's an essential part to running but most of the time it's pretty much there as a safety precaution. At times, water is an essential part to running or playing sport, for example, I used to go out and play football with my best friend Chris and my brother. I remember sweating so much and not drinking that I blanked out and I couldn't see a thing. I was crossing the road at the same time too and remember shouting to my brother that I couldn't see. Of course my brother shook his shoulders and was a bit confused, I think he thought I was lying but I wasn't, I couldn't see a thing. There have been other times this has happened too, I remember going on the cross trainer we had in the house and training so hard, I hadn't eaten because we were going out for a meal at TGI Fridays. I kept having to ask for pints of water at TGI Fridays to stop me blanking out I had trained so hard.

So, water is an essential item in running but many people drink too much which I guess is the safer option to blanking out and not being able to see a thing!

GYM

If I had to be honest, I hate this place; it's a place where I pushed myself to the brink. There just doesn't seem to be a way of getting the "feel good" factor in the gym, there seems to be so much strain you put on your heart in the gym, that's why I prefer running outside. In fact, I used to be one of two people left in the gym at 9pm every weekday because I knew if I kept up my running and fitness I could win races. Unfortunately, I pushed myself too hard and ended up in hospital. You see, like I've said before, commitment is a key trait for people with Aspergers. Once they start something they are committed, just like I was with my running, I was committed but it made me ill.

"I hate the gym so much."

I hate the gym, saying that though the gym can be a place to meet new people, a place where you can get that "feel good" factor through meeting new people, not just by exercising. Having Aspergers it can be hard to find new friends though, starting a conversation is incredibly difficult, I mean what do you talk about, I mean you're in the gym to train, not to talk. It can become easier though, maybe I should create a kind of script I can use to talk and meet up with new people at the gym.

RELIGION

"Am I religious?" well that's a tough question to answer; I mean what is being "religious"? Officially I'm a Catholic, so I have a strong religious upbringing; I used to go to church every other Sunday and was brought up in a religious primary and secondary school. I tend to think of myself as being open to all sorts of religions, I know I'm a Catholic but I don't tend to follow the faith and advice many Catholic's preach. Some of the stories you hear in the Bible aren't the most believable either, I mean turning water into wine, Jesus could have easily been a magician, a person who fooled many crowds.

"Am I really religious?"

After my psychosis, I'm prepared to start visiting churches more often as it's certainly made me more of a religious person. I mean I wouldn't want to go to church every week but once a month would certainly be viable. You see churches are social places too, so I can make friends through the church.

To put it simply, I believe that when we die we go into another body, in other words reincarnation. Whether that is a dog, cat or another human, it's the most obvious thing to believe you see. When we die, our brains shut down but we must move to another brain, obviously we don't know it, it's not an obvious thing because our brains are all different. If I had to choose a religion, that's what I'd believe.

BLOG EXTRACT: BELIEVE YOU CAN AND YOU WILL

Two weeks ago I wrote a blog saying this was going to be the biggest mental challenge of my life and it is, but I'm through the worst, I'm feeling like I'm back, back to the Dan we all know. Yesterday, I finished a 10k in 46 minutes, my belief is back, today I'm feeling okay…ish, but I know it will take time, there's going to be days where I get more anxious than others, but what I've done is reduce my anxiety down to a teeny, tiny, worm, what I've done is BELIEVE.

I go on and on about believing in yourself, through times of struggle, when you're at your lowest of lows, can you crawl yourself out of that hole and become even stronger. Just last week I was in severe mental pain, crawled on my bed clenching a red nose, it felt there was no way out, my anxiety was through the roof, every time I lost focus, I just started shaking, I was crying at everything, the day's felt like a month, I had never experienced this kind anxiety before.

The most amazing thing is, I was knew to this, I didn't have clue how to control it, but I believed, I believed I could beat this thing, I sit here today having pretty much beaten it. Now I want this to be as easy for you as possible, if you're really struggling with anxiety at the minute. I'm putting together what I'm calling a 20 point plan to battling and most importantly reducing anxiety. I know it's different for everyone but by following these simple coping strategies it will help you, just like they've helped me. Please share the image above on social media, whilst direct them to this blog, where I explain more.

Don't Panic – This will only make you more anxious, try and relax.

Connection – Talk about your feelings with family and friends.

Emotion – Let it all out, cry as much as you want, feel the world.

Sensory Box – Smell, taste, hear, create a sensory box.

Water – Drink plenty of water, drink slowly, focus on each gulp.

Food – Eat slowly and focus on every single bite you take.

Music – This drives you, Spotify have good Anxiety Relief playlists.

Get Outside -Feel the wind, bask in the sun, breath, senses relax you.

Exercise – Important, at least 30 minutes a day.

Run – If you can go for a run, scream as loud as you want, let it all out.

Go Easy – You can't do as much as you used to do, that's OKAY.

Live In The Moment – Feeling anxious, focus on a task.

Video Games – I bought a Nintendo Switch Lite to focus on.

Cut Out Caffeine – No Alcohol, coke or caffeine, you can do this.

No Smoking – It's a drug, you may think it's relaxing you, but it's not.

No Swearing – Avoid swearing as much as possible.

Sleep – Can't sleep, don't sweat, plug some headphones in and chill.

Breath – Google Wim Hoff, breath slowly, focus on every single breath.

Time – Take each day as slow as you want to, don't worry about time.

Believe – Most importantly, believe, remember #anythingispossible.

Big hugs X

Dan

FOOD

Ask any runner, they'll tell you, you can eat anything if you run, a McDonald's Breakfast, a bucket full of chicken from KFC or an XL Bacon Double Cheeseburger from Burger King. I love eating food, it's a reward after a long, rainy, hard run. In fact, I thought I'd write a specific section on food just to reveal my love for the stuff.

First up, it has to be my favourite of all the foods, it's McDonalds, I used to go their every Thursday before everything become locked down. Every Thursday or every other Thursday, don't want to make me seem totally like a pig, I used to go to McDonalds with my Dad and we used to have a feast. I used to use my student card to get a free cheeseburger or Mayo Chicken, there's something about things being free. My favourite burger in McDonalds has to be the Grand Big Mac or the Big Tasty. Ordering food isn't that scary anymore either as McDonalds has self-ordering tills you can order food on, so there are no awkward conversations between you and the cashier. Well it isn't that scary anyway, that's just my Aspergers kicking in. In fact I can ask, I know the menu off by heart, just take a look at some of the menu items I've listed from memory:

"I know the McDonalds menu by hand."

Big Mac – small, medium or large. Nothing but large exists completely in my eyes.

Grand Big Mac – When available order this, it's bigger better and don't forget to get the one with bacon.

Big Tasty (With Bacon) – of course you have to choose bacon, that's the best burger, the sauce is awesome too.

Chicken Nuggets – Choose the share box, nothing else but 20 nuggets to tuck into between yourself.

If you haven't watched that film about McDonalds, it's called "The Founder", you need too. Did you know? McDonalds is the biggest toy shop in the world, its fast food technique emerged from a tennis court and its main attraction to its burgers is the sauce. In terms of its advertising; I love it when McDonalds do the Monopoly campaign. It's such a clever idea encouraging you to buy more stuff and win free food, well most of the time it's free food, I wish it was the money though, £100,000 imagine what you could do with that. I've been looking for Mayfair for a while though it just doesn't pop up on the back of my quarter pounder. I could widdle on about

McDonalds for ages, the food, the sauce, the toys, oh and not forgetting the land they own. McDonalds own literally loads of land and that's why they are everywhere in cities and town centres.

Burger King is next on my list of food to eat. At Burger King there's only one burger you have to choose, it's the XL Bacon Double Cheese Burger. It's so juicy and fresh. Unlike McDonalds where the burgers aren't all real meat, Burger King is real. The gooey bacon and cheese inside the burger is so amazing, cheesy and big. The chips at Burger King are crispy too but they have to have ketchup with them, I don't like Burger King's chips with no ketchup, they just don't taste right. Burger King's burgers also contain real meat, that's the difference between McDonalds and Burger King.

"You have to choose the XL Double Bacon Cheeseburger."

Moving on to KFC, now this is a takeaway for sharing. I mean, imagine someone getting a mop bucket, filling it up with 20 or so pieces of chicken, fried in the colonel's favourite recipe and say eat it. That's KFC, it's for sharing, you can eat it on your own, it just depends on how much of a pig you are. The only thing I don't like about KFC is the sticky fingers; you always get sticky fingers when you eat it. This bothers me every time I eat, that's my OCD, how on earth do you clean your fingers filled with grease? What about if your phone is just about to slip out of your pocket, you have sticky fingers, what on earth do you do? The only option is to save your phone, risk your phone getting sticky, otherwise you'll be without a phone because if that phone hits the ground, it will shatter into one billion pieces, I'll have no way to contact anyone and I will die, a long and winding death with no one there to support me. Of course, I won't, that's just my OCD way of thinking, my phone will just get a bit sticky.

Moving on from a rather sticky scenario, let's talk about Dominos. I used to order a pizza for myself every Saturday and you know what, I think I might order myself one again. There's only one option with Dominos, stuffed crust, BBQ base, lots of lots of sour cream dip and of course the cookies for pudding.

"You can't forget about Pizza."

Pizza Hut comes next in my food journey. Now Pizza Hut is a tricky takeaway, they have good pizza, I especially like the cream base but I've never really had them as a takeaway, I've always sat inside. So I'm going to say

Pizza Hut is more restaurant material. I love sitting in at Pizza Hut, I especially like the free salad you get at the start. Mmm, lots of carbs to fill you up before you eat more carbs in the form of pizza. As well as the salad, I love the Ice Cream Factory for desert, this is supposed to be for kids but that doesn't bother me. The prospect of eating unlimited ice cream is too much not to take, I love eating ice cream especially the Mr Whippy type of ice cream, it has something about it that makes it beautiful, creamy and soft.

Pizza Express is another restaurant on my list I need to talk about, this restaurant is more on the posh side of the pizza places. I love the dough balls and the fresh pizza bases the restaurant is famous for. I went there for New Year last year with my sister and her boyfriend, it was a good meal out. It's the kind of restaurant you'd imagine "Lady" sitting in, if it was a Lady & The Tramp movie. I can just imagine a dog, sharing spaghetti with another dog at a table. It's funny isn't it, how the media change your perception of a restaurant, how can fine dining in Pizza Express make you think of two dogs sharing spaghetti, in fact what dog would actually be willing to share a piece of spaghetti, most dogs I know, that's not many by the way, would scoff spaghetti straight down.

"Mexican to Indian, there's a lot of takeaways to choose from."

The next restaurant I love is Chiquito's. I've only been their once but my brother Harry loves going there. It's a Mexican restaurant and I really enjoyed it when I went to eat there. The only thing that lets it down is the portion sizes, they could be bigger but I'm not bothered how much food you get, what I've realised is that it's not the food portions that's important, it's the flavour of the food you should be more aware off. Chiquito's food taste amazing, I especially love the Halloumi cheese and the Mexican flavour in the wraps. If you fancy a taste adventure, try Chiquitos.

A similar type of restaurant is Nando's, well they market themselves as similar, despite one being a Mexican restaurant and the other being Portuguese. They both have similar aesthetic in their advertising and of course, they both serve chicken. At Nandos I often choose the half chicken with the lemon and herb dressing. You have to choose the lemon and herb dressing, it's so tasty, next time I go though, I might opt for the mango dressing. I love the unlimited drinks in Nando's too, it's especially useful if you're going to try all of the spicy dressings as you need a drink to get rid of the extreme heat let off by the spicy Nando sauce.

Belle Italia comes next on my list of favourite restaurants. Belle Italia are once again pitched towards the fine dining kind of restaurants. They're more like a Pizza Express. I always imagine a man playing piano in the corner whilst you're eating at Pizza Express. In fact, whilst we've been on lockdown, I made my living room into a bit of a Pizza Express/Belle Italia restaurant. I downloaded some "man playing piano" music and played it on my Bluetooth speaker in the corner of the room. It was just like being at the restaurant except for the wooden table and the endless washing up to do.

"I always choose the Lamb Tikka Masala."

There's something about an Indian takeaway that gives it a worthy place in this book. I was introduced to the magic of the curry when I went out for a curry night with my work. I wasn't sure what to order at first, after all I was new on the curry scene, I used to think that all curry was hot and spicy and so I stayed away from it completely. I know what you're thinking, that's so stereotypical, I know it is, it's very stereotypical. After visiting the Indian, I loved the experience; the food is an explosion of flavour, especially the Lamb Tikka Masala, which isn't hot or spicy after all. I honestly don't know why you would go to a curry house to just sweat, what's the point in eating something that makes you sweat as much as you would running the London Marathon. I mean, you're even given a hot towel to wipe the sweat off your forehead at the end. It's not the just the curry, the naan bread, I particularly love Peshwari naan, a lot of people say it's too sweet, but I don't think it is, I think it's perfect, after all I've got a sweet tooth.

Talking of sweets things, one thing I haven't covered is chocolate. If I had to choose between chocolate and sweets I'd probably choose chocolate, it' so much tastier and addictive. I'm a lover of Cadbury's chocolate, especially Dairy Milk, I bought myself a giant Dairy Milk bar for Easter, it was over 800 grams of pure milky chocolate, it was so delicious, I actually eat it all whilst I was in this mental health hospital. Other chocolate that comes top of my list is Kinder Beuno or a Kinder Surprise, as a kid I used to love opening up the toy inside the egg to see what toy I had, I still do to this day, that's why my Mum calls me a big kid.

"I'm getting rather hungry now."

I promise this is the last paragraph I write on food, I know I could go on all day and I've probably made you hungry too. So I'll finish up talking about by ultimate meal, if I could eat a three meals, breakfast, lunch and dinner for the rest of my life what would I choose. The first thing I'd choose has to be porridge for Breakfast, I mean there's nothing better than waking up to a bowl of hot gooey, thick porridge in the morning. It's even better if you add bananas to it or some granola or you could opt for some maple syrup. Next on the list is a lasagne for lunch, I love the sauces you get with it, it's so creamy, the sauce tastes divine and when you combine it with the pasta and the meat, it's even more delicious. I wouldn't have chips with the lasagne as I'd be too full to eat what's on my plate at dinner. To finish up at dinner, I'd choose a roast, there's nothing better than goose fat potatoes, carrots, broccoli alongside a tender lamb joint, plus some apple crumble for pudding.

BLOG EXTRACT: A LETTER TO AN 18 YEAR OLD DAN

Dear Dan,

I'm sat here in my bedroom writing this on my 28th birthday. I know you're 18 years old, about to go to university, not knowing what to expect, what you're going to do with your life but don't be scared, go to university and face every challenge head on, stay focused and achieve your dreams.

Believe

Anything is possible Dan, one thing I've learnt over 28 years is that whatever you want to do, you can do it. If you want to learn guitar, learn another language, write a best selling book or run a marathon, it's possible. I recently lost six stone in 10 months because I believed it was possible. If you go through life with this mentality you're bound to succeed. It's all about thinking positively.

Break Out Of Your Comfort Zone

Another thing, break out of your comfort zone. If you wake up at the same time everyday, sit at your work desk doing the same thing, go home, eat dinner and then sleep and you do this day in, day out, you're likely to start feeling down and most likely suffer a form of depression or anxiety.

If you go to work and think, what can I do that will challenge myself today, you'll start opening new doors and windows of opportunity, you would have never experienced beforehand. I recently organised a raffle as part of my London Marathon fundraising, I had to go into stores and ask if they'd like to offer me a raffle prize. Of course I wasn't comfortable but I learnt from it and each time I visited a store, I came feeling more and more confident. I've taken up running too, this has made me feel a lot more confident, I would never thought I'd run a marathon 10 years ago.

Be Different

As humans we follow each other like a tribe, we're constantly being told what we should do, wear, say and eat. Break free from this, be yourself. As a runner myself, I get up early every Saturday and run a 15 mile or more run. On a Sunday I'm one of 10 cars on the road heading to the gym whilst everyone's tucked up in bed recovering from a hangover from the night before. This is what I mean by being different, don't let anyone tell you what you should or shouldn't be doing.

Yours Faithfully

Dan Jones

(The 28 Year Old Version)

PS Happy Birthday To Me!

NANNY AND GRAMPY

I always feel good when I visit my Nanny & Grampy. I'm lucky enough to have two sets of grandparents, one on the Jones side and the other on the Allen side. Now, the Allen side is actually called the Shutford side, just to confuse you even more, we call my Nan, Nan Shutford because she lives in Shutford and we used to go and visit her and see all the animals in Shutford. Shutford is a small village in Oxfordshire, it's not a surname before you get even more confused. So I have two sides, the Jones and the Shutford side.

There's something unique and comforting about visiting older people, they just seem to offer support, comfort and guidance. A lot of the time throughout my life I've gone to my Grampy Jones for help and assistance, especially if it's about my car. See, my Grampy Jones used to work in a local garage, I bought my car from that garage and so I often find it comforting to ask him questions about my car even though the only thing he knows about cars is the accounting side of things. It's this comfort and guidance that makes older people special. Sadly I recently lost my Grampy Jones, he was an amazing person and worked really hard. I'll miss him so much and that support and guidance has now gone although I can turn to my Nan or my other set of Grandparents.

I often find it's easier to talk to older people than younger people, I just find the conversation flows better. I just find older people speak a lot slower than younger people, so my brain can process the thought a lot easier whereas younger people often talk pretty fast. I'm not saying I can't communicate with younger people, I just find a lot of youngers don't have the same interests as me.

"There's always something special about visiting Grandparents."

I love my grandparents cooking too, not that I don't love my Mum and Dad's cooking. There's something magical about visiting your Grandparents for dinner. Imagine, tucking into a succulent roast, crispy roast potatoes, goose fat burnt parsnips and buttered carrots. If you're not visiting for a roast, you could be visiting to have cake. I love my Nan's cakes or deserts for that matter, butter creamed cakes, apple crumble or chocolate pie. Now, chocolate pie is a very unique recipe and it runs a lot within the family. It's a mixture of butter, cocoa powder and corn flower, mixed together to make a chocolate looking pie. The base is smashed biscuits with butter. Anyway, if food is on the equation, whatever you get it's guaranteed to be delicious.

So, I've talked about who my Grandparents are, what you get when you visit them a.k.a food, now it's time to talk about the time you visit them. See, visiting my grandparents always takes place at a certain time. When I was younger I visited my Nan and Grampy Jones on a Tuesday after school, I saw my Nan Shutford every Saturday afternoon. Now I'm older I see my Nan and Grampy Jones on a Wednesday after work for one hour, I see my Nan Shutford every other weekend on a Saturday afternoon. I'm telling you this because the times I visited my Nan and Grampy are precious, I remember every single bit about visiting them. I remember my Nan picking me up from primary school and taking us to a park to play. I remember the school holidays, where we used to go to a park and pick blackberries from the field. My Nan used to look after my cousins too, Ryan and Dominic and we used to go and play in what we used to call Dinosaur Land.

"I used to love blackberry picking."

We used to explore in the woods, run around and use our imagination. As a kid we used our imagination excessively and it's something a lot of adults forget. I think running helps with your imagination as you're constantly running through new places, exploring and looking for new things. I wish more adults had a better imagination, I get really angry when people say they won't watch a film because it is computer generated. I mean do you know how long it's taken the artists, the designers, the computer experts to create that film, people forget that the people that created that animated film are adults, they are not kids, they have an imagination.

Anyway rant over, we used to go and play in the woods and it really was a magical time. I used to go to my Nan Jones every Tuesday. I remember one day coming home and the news came on the TV, two planes had gone into the twin towers in New York. I stood at the TV in awe at what was going on. My Nan said this would be history and it is still to this day, the 9/11 attack which killed so many, I was just a child when it happened and my Nan was right, it had gone down in history.

See, it's these memories we treasure forever that's why I'm writing this book because I want to remember my life to the best I can. Spending time with my

Grandparents is so special, as I said when I started this chapter, spending time with Grandparents is unique, comforting and special and I've clearly demonstrated this in this chapter.

WORK

You know I have Aspergers so you're probably expecting this part to be quite short, it's not, in fact it's actually one of the longest chapters of the book. I've excelled in the workplace but after struggling with my mental health and being in this mental health hospital I've sadly had to leave my position with VTUK. See, the pressure of work has really got to me after suffering a psychotic episode it's proving a real challenge to hold down a job. I would say to someone with autism that they can do anything if they put their mind to it, just like I have been able to do.

Anyway, I used to work for VTUK (Vision Teknology United Kingdom). They are an estate agency/letting agency solution provider and I am in charge of their marketing and social media. They do estate agency and letting agency software solutions and I do their social media, so if you're an estate agent looking for new software don't be afraid to give them a call on 01865 860870, there you have it a blatant advert in my book, I'll make sure they pay me for that, only joking. Many people phone up and think they're BTUK, a lot of people phone up and think they're talking to BT instead of VTUK, I guess it's an easy mistake to make.

"VTUK came to my rescue."

I remember when I first went to the interview for my job, I met a man called Pete, I went into the interview having my key phrases ready. See before going into an interview , I like to rehearse what I am going to say, I remember a bit about the company, my 3 key skills and what I am good at and my previous education and employment. Having Aspergers I find it difficult to find the conversation in interviews so I have to set out key points and refer back to them during the interview process. Back before I started at VTUK, I perfected my CV, as I'm good at writing out my work experience, what I am not good at is then explaining it all in a social scene. The only way for me to have a good interview is for me to have pre-planned questions, ready for me to answer.

That's when VTUK came to rescue, I actually was offered two positions on the same day, one by a LGBT company (Micro Rainbow International) in London but this was part time and the other with VTUK. I took VTUK's offer as this was a full time opportunity and I couldn't turn it away. They had made the job for me as I had made them realise how important social media is for their business. I had sold them the job of social media management and my career in social media began.

I remember my first day at VTUK, I wanted to impress them from the get-go, I went in to the office all guns blazing, I wanted to make this company huge, massive and global across the social media airwaves. That's my Aspergers see, if I believe I can do something, I will, like I'm writing this book, I'm believing this book will be published, it will be bigger than some top sellers, it will help other people struggling with Aspergers or people with Aspergers. That's a positive trait with someone with Aspergers, they will sit down and believe they can do something. Anyway, back to my first day, I literally impressed them from the moment I walked in the door and I still do to this day.

"I often feel frustrated when the phone rings."

One thing I get a bit annoyed about is answering the phone at work, I often feel frustrated when the phone rings I have to wait for someone to pick it up. One thing I need to accept is that I cannot answer the phone like other people can. I need to start thinking kindly of myself now, especially as I write this with just 3 weeks gone after coming out of hospital. I need to accept answering and communicating with people is a weakness, I can't do it as effectively as some people can.

That's no means a problem as I can help other people in other ways, for example I am an expert at planning a conversation, so I can help the sales team with communicating the right way and that's exactly why I do social media. It's because social media allows me to communicate in a certain way but it allows me thinking time which you don't have when you communicate verbally. I think it's quite ironic, me being a social media expert when I struggle to communicate in everyday life. I mean I have a degree in Communication when that's the one thing I struggle doing, day in, day out.

My boss at work has been so, so supportive of me throughout my psychotic episode. He's really understood what I've been going through which has really helped my recovery. One thing I like about work is how we are all family, in fact we market ourselves as the VTUK Tribe. You have the mum of the pack, the dad of the pack, the brothers, sisters, the young ones and the older ones. Each one of us at VTUK plays a part in the team and we treat each other with respect. That's why I love my boss at work because he treats everyone equal and he'll be amazed at my story within this book, he'll be reading this right now thinking 'how on earth does Dan live his day to day life?'. I mean I've managed though; it's so difficult having Aspergers, not knowing what confirms to the norms of society, in fact what actually is normal? What is a normal way of living? The normal way of speaking? The normal way of cooking? We go about our daily lives and people accept a normal way of behaviour, but the truth is, there is no normal way of living. We live in different cultures across the world, there is no normal.

Anyway back on to the subject of my boss, he's the best because he doesn't think of himself as a boss, as I said above, he thinks of himself as family. Throughout my 6 years at VTUK he's recognised that he needs to embed himself in VTUK as a team player, a person you can go to at times of difficulty and that's why he's the best boss in the world because he's been there for me throughout my time at VTUK. He recognises that I've need extra support at social events because I struggle communicating, so he's allowed me to invite my sister along so I have someone I know there to talk to. He's recognised I need support around me in the workplace so he's situated me next to the Office Manager who I can talk to for support anytime I need it, he's always coming up to me to ask if I need help or assistance at work, that's because he cares, he knows the difficulties I go through on a day to day basis.

Just going to talk to a colleague is difficult for me which would be so easy for anyone else. I push through though because, I believe. That's why I'm sat here right know hammering words out because I believe this book will be published, it will be a bestseller because it will help others struggling with Aspergers, autism and show others what LIFE really means.

THEME PARKS

I love going to a theme park, I'll go on anything, whether it goes upside down, round and round, left or right, I'll be on it. There is an exception though, I won't go on anything scary; I hate scary rides like haunted houses or scare mazes. My imagination is wild so that's probably why I hate scary rides so much, I mean having psychosis is the scariest thing I've ever been through, I mean I've literally been living in a nightmare which should make going on scary rides easier, but it doesn't.

"I Love Theme Parks."

Choosing my favourite theme park is such a difficult decision. They are all so different, for example, Alton Towers is a family friendly park, it's full of extremely well themed rides which are all magical. It has the backdrop of the towers too which makes it even more magical. Then there's Thorpe Park which is aimed more at adults as a lot of the rides at the park are extreme, fast and thrill-seeking. Chessington is once again a family friendly place which has well themed rides too, like the Tomb Blaster where you go into a tomb and battle against a giant snake and werewolf. Last, but not least is Legoland. Legoland's mainly aimed at children under 12 as the rides are gentler and it pitches itself as a place full of Lego.

If I had to choose one, I'd say Alton Towers is my favourite, it's the best theme park to visit as it's such a special and enchanting place. I mean they market themselves as a place of adventure, a place of thrills, wonder and magic. That's why I love Alton Towers so much, they want you to go and enjoy a magical day out. That's exactly how I think, I want to go to a theme park to explore, have fun and enjoy a magical day. Alton Towers has it all, it has a huge tower, an amazing back story and amazingly brilliant themed rides.

"Alton Towers Is Magical."

My favourite ride at Alton Towers has to be The Smiler. It's such a good ride, there are so many loops and it's brilliantly themed. Think about the name for a minute, "The Smiler". It's asking you to smile on a ride that's tossing and turning you through no end of loops, it's so ironic. Yet, when adults go on the rollercoaster they turn into a kid again, they want to be enchanted, they want to be thrilled and they smile. That's why I can't understand the people who are scared to go on rollercoasters, the amount of people you see smiling on a ride, they're not being sick, they are enjoying themselves. It's such a shame that The Smiler has got a bad reputation in the news though, the ride is brilliant, but a lot of people are afraid to ride it due to the crash that took place on it. It took two people's legs off and changed their life forever.

My favourite time of year to visit Alton Towers is during Bonfire Night. I love the fireworks display Alton Towers puts on. The back drop is the two towers and the fireworks look magnificent going off in front of them. The fireworks run to a timer and sync with the music amazingly well. It's so cold too, so when you're looking up at the fireworks whilst feeling nice and toasty in your coat or chilly without a coat, it all depends on if you remembered one, it's such an amazing feeling.

Another thing I love is the idea of going to the funfair. The local Bob Willis funfair arrives in Banbury every third week in October. Lorry after lorry along with caravan after caravan makes its way into the centre of Banbury to unload their ride. I find it amazing how each lorry is filled with a ride, it's incredible how 200 or so travellers go from town to town giving hundreds of people enjoyment and fun. I mean some of the rides are huge, some are taller than the Banbury town hall and still they manage to travel from town to town.

One thing funfairs do have a bad reputation for is their safety standards. I know the funfair isn't as safe as a Theme Park, which is maintained on a daily basis, funfairs move around on a lorry and aren't as well looked after. That doesn't stop me though, life is for living , I'm not going to be scared of a ride dropping me from thin air, life is for taking risks and I'm not going to miss out on enjoyment just because funfairs have poor safety standards.

RUNNING

Let's talk more about me and my running. Many people ask me what I did to start running, many people ask me to write about what I did to actually get motivated to run 3, 5 or 10 miles for the first time. Well, it simply was my brain saying I'm going to run this distance now and off I went. That was it, just pure belief that I would get out and run that specific distance. Now I'm recovering from being in a mental health hospital and I'm having to start from scratch again, I'm having to bring that belief back again because I've lost confidence and fitness to run the half marathon distance. Yet again, I'm believing but this time I've got to be very careful, very, very careful because the thing is, I made myself ill last time. I put too much pressure on myself to perform at the highest level. This time I'm taking it easy and seeing how things go. So far I've ran 4 miles, many people would struggle to run 4 miles but the simple fact is that they are lazy. You can run any distance if you choose to, you simple just have to believe it's possible, alright it might take a lot longer than elite runners but you can run the distance if you put that belief attitude into practice.

One thing I write about a lot on my blog is mindset, having the right mindset is huge in everything you do in life, not just running or exercise but in everything. I'm sat here writing this book having to concentrate so hard on every single word I'm typing. I'm concentrating not because I need to concentrate but because my brain is struggling from a psychotic episode. That's the belief I have you see, anyone else sat here would be struggling but I never give in, I've written a 30,000 word book simply by believing and having the right mindset.

TWITTER

One thing I've not mentioned yet is my Twitter community, they're a real inspiring bunch. I thought I'd give a couple of shout outs so here goes, shout out's too.

@TheRealMelHeale
@JimbotheRunner
@RunningLikeEh
@runtalkrun
@Babsytherunner

I love Twitter so much in fact I think I'm pretty much addicted. Out of all the social media platforms I think Twitter is the best as it's so easy to find information, in other words it's more of a news site than a social media platform. Anyway, enough of me wittering on about social media, this book isn't a media theory book it's about my life, my life living with Aspergers.

RUN TALK RUN

Ever stepped out of your comfort zone? I have several times in my life and I find it challenging but once you've done it, it feels amazing. One example when I took the plunge and decided to go out of my comfort zone was when I chose to become a Run Leader for Run Talk Run in my local area. I chose to become a Run Talk Run Leader because I had become so much more confident through my running. Running had given me much greater confidence to handle telephone calls and manage a group, plus I like new challenges and this was going to be one.

"I like stepping out of my comfort zone."

Run Talk Run is an organisation set up by Jessica Robson, I first learned of them on social media and contacted her to become a run leader. I saw her talk at the National Running Show where she explained how she had Belimier and had used running to help her recover. She used to run to burn calories knowing the calories she'd burnt could be consumed later on by eating, running effectively saved her life.

Anyway, back to my story, at the beginning I kept thinking "how was I going to manage a group of runners with my Aspergers?". This ran round in my head at the beginning as I wasn't at all confident, I struggle to communicate myself let alone communicate with other people. I put this thought to one side though and thought about the times I had led a group, for example whilst I was at University and during my job. I was scared to begin with in these situations but I did it because I put myself in the right mindset. If you're reading this with Aspergers/ autism now I'd say to start trying new things, break boundaries as you can do anything if you simply believe.

Anyway, I did it, I organised my first ever running group and led the group to run 5k! I learnt so much from the run, it's amazing how good running can feel when you run with no pressure, no time, just you and others to talk to.

BLOG EXTRACT: MY FIRST RUN TALK RUN

I did it, I organised my first ever running group and led the group to run 5k! I learnt so much from the run, it's amazing how good running can feel when you run with no pressure, no time, just you and others to talk to.

When We First Arrived

I have to be honest, when I first arrived at Middleton Cheney Library I really thought nobody was going to turn up. Me, my mum, her boyfriend and my brothers were literally about to go until we saw some people arrive. It was amazing when I saw faces, setting up my running group suddenly felt worthwhile, I was inspiring others to run and beat there mental health. In fact, it was the longest some of them had run in a long time, incredibly my Mum even ran, just last year she couldn't even walk due to her Transverse Myelitis, let alone run, it was amazing to see!

A Sense Of Connection

When we started running, I wasn't sure how fast to run, I know I'm a lot fitter than the average runner so I was careful not to go steaming ahead. Once we got going though we started talking about all sorts, I suddenly completely forget I was running and started talking, confidently as well, about my running journey and my life. It was amazing being able to share my journey whilst running, just having someone there with me whilst I run with no pressure, just the outside world and the time passing by was incredible.

HOLIDAYS

There's always something special about going on HOLIDAY, in other words going on an ADVENTURE, going somewhere DIFFERENT, MAGICAL, AMAZING and SPECIAL. These words pop into my mind when I hear the word holiday. Holidays are a chance to go to a new destination and explore the area, find fascinating things about a different place. A lot of people nowadays think holidays are a chance to relax and take time out; I think completely the opposite when I think of the holiday. I think relaxing is for other times in your life, if you're going to go to a new place, why not explore the area and make the most of being away. What's the point in going to a beach and sitting there all day and not doing anything, it's pointless; I really don't understand the people who do this. See, my brain is busy, it's extremely active so relaxation holidays are a big no-no on my holiday list, I just get bored. That's why I'm really struggling recovering from this psychotic episode, I like being active and always on the go. At the minute my brain's struggling to get going which is frustrating me but as the days go by, things are getting easier and easier.

"Holidays Have Always Been Magic."

Most of my holidays have taken place across the UK throughout my childhood as my parents couldn't afford to take us abroad, that doesn't mean I didn't enjoy them, I loved visiting all sorts of different caravan parks. The first thing that comes to mind when I think of our caravan holidays is Haven and their mascots Rory The Tiger, Anxious The Elephant and Greedy The Gorilla. They used to come on stage in the evening and do party dances, I remember the lyrics still to this day. They went something like "we're looking for tigers and big alligators; we're having fun in the tiger club.". The Tiger Club was a children's club, we didn't attend it though as it meant talking to other children and me being shy and having Aspergers thought it would be better to stay with the security of my parents.

The mascots aren't the only thing I can remember about Haven, I remember being scared of a clown at a camp in the Isle of White once. It ran into the audience and almost put a cream pie on my face.

We went on many trips whilst at Haven parks too, including to the beach. Now I'm not a lover of the beach, it's sandy and wet, and if you haven't realised yet sand and water don't mix. Sand gets all on your feet and you simply can't get it off. That's why I hate the beach, I like the sea though, I've always been a strong swimmer and swimming in the sea is what I do like. It takes a while for me to adjust to the beach setting. See, when you arrive at the beach you have to place a towel on the floor, once the towel is on the floor you need to find a way to get dressed into your swimming trunks without getting sand everywhere. See, this is my OCD, if one bit of sand touches my socks that's the end of the world, one grain and it's all over. Now you can see why I hate the beach, it's a nightmare for people with OCD like me.

The beach wasn't the only place we went on our Haven breaks. I remember the World's Strongest Man was being filmed one day whilst we were on a campsite. It was shown the next day on TV, I couldn't see myself though. We went to Crealy Adventure Park once too, where we went on slides and all sorts of adventure park stuff. My favourite place to visit whilst on holiday was Flambards. This was right down near the bottom of Cornwall. Flambards had all sorts of thrills you could experience. As well as the rides, Flambards had a Victorian Street you could walk down. The street had shops with replica Victorian items in them. It was like a museum but within a theme park setting. If I could choose one place to go back to, it would be Flambards. Travelling forward through the years, my Mum eventually split up with my Dad, so we often went on two UK holidays a year. This was a bonus as it meant we got to see more of the UK in a year and got the benefit of two holidays rather than one.

My holidays haven't just been in the UK, since growing up I've paid to go to some incredible places around the world. I've visited America twice, Orlando a.k.a Universal Studios and Las Vegas, Tenerife, Malaga and Torremolinos.

"I've travelled the world too."

My first trip to America was incredible; I went with my Sister to Universal Studios, Orlando. I've always wanted to go here as I'm a huge Harry Potter fan. They have a themed area dedicated to Harry Potter so this trip was a huge achievement for me. It wasn't just Harry Potter that attracted me to this holiday, it was going to America. I was going to see a huge country which is plastered in every bit of media we consume here in the UK. If you think about it American culture is littered in the media we consume, from food advertising to the food we eat to the TV and films we watch. That's why I wanted to go to America to see what I've been consuming all these years.

We flew from Birmingham Airport to Orlando; my Mum drove us to the airport where we started the holiday with an airport lounge. We had toast, yoghurts and mini cans of Diet Coke for Breakfast before we set off on our flight. The plane we were travelling in was the Dreamliner, one of TUI's newest model aircrafts. These planes were special as the windows could be dimmed down, it had mood lighting in the cabin and we had a TV set to watch movies and play games on. I've never been on a plane for over 20 years so I couldn't really compare it with anything else but it was pretty cool. I remember me and my Sister playing "Who Wants To Be A Millionaire?" on the TV set and watching Gone Girl, a new movie that had just come out. Anyway, the plane was cool but that was just the start of the holiday.

When we arrived in Orlando I remember feeling a gust of hot air as I walked out of the plane, it felt almost like a sauna. As soon as I felt that hot air, I knew this was going to be a hot holiday. I don't like the heat for two reasons, number one you sweat all day which means you need to put your clothes to the wash and number two, you simply feel tired and can't be bothered to do anything. I knew this was going to be a test for me when

I first stepped out of the plane but I was prepared. I had brought a hat with me as well as some sun cream. I hate putting sun cream on though, it's like having to plaster yourself with white paint, I really didn't enjoy putting it on everyday but I wanted to come and see this amazing theme park, Universal Studios, so I did what needed to be done.

We arrived at the hotel and had a look around; it was called "Cabana Bay" and was themed around the 1960s. There was 60s decoration, a 60s themed bowling alley, it even had some food packaging designed around the 60s. We had an onsite bus that could take us to the theme parks, which was really handy.

"Orlando was an amazing experience."

The first thing we did was buy our park tickets. This meant waiting in a queue line in the blistering heat for ages. By the time we collected the tickets it was time to go and find something to eat. We headed to an area outside the theme parks called Universal Downtown. Downtown had all sorts of restaurants, shops and bars you could go into, plus an interactive mini-golf course you could play. For the first night, we decided we'd grab a hotdog from a hotdog restaurant. This wasn't just any hotdog though, this was an America hotdog, it had tons of bacon bits, cheese and onions on it and it was huge. That was the start of our food journey in America.

The next couple of days saw us exploring the two main Universal theme parks. We started our second day by going on the Simpsons ride. Now this was no ordinary ride, in fact all of the rides at Universal Studios are incredible. This particular ride, the Simpsons ride had an area you walked down where the scene was set for you, after watching a short clip from the Simpsons you boarded a car. You're then greeted to a giant IMAX screen, it's that big it feels like you're actually with the Simpsons. A lot of the rides are developed in a similar way at Universal Studios, you start the ride watching a clip from whatever ride you're riding and then you board a car and you're taken on an amazing adventure. This is cleverly done as a lot of the rides are indoors which means when it thunders the rides don't have to shut down.

My favourite themed area was of course the Harry Potter section of the theme park. I'm a lover of Harry Potter, I grew up with it as a child and If you read the chapter on my bedroom, you'll know my bedroom is decorated in a Harry Potter theme. In fact, we broke down on the Gringotts ride, if you're not familiar with Harry Potter, Gringotts is a bank in Harry Potter, it's where all the vaults are and in this ride you go into the vaults and you see all the characters in an incredible 3D motion ride. Unfortunately, we broke down on the second time of riding it. The troll was supposed to throw us but we suddenly stopped. I was wondering what was going on at first and then I realised after 20 minutes of no movement and the lights coming on, that we had broken down. We waited for an hour and we were escorted off the ride. I wasn't too scared because I knew the mechanics knew what they were doing. All the Harry Potter rides were mind boggling and crazily good, another ride used a Japanese robotic arm, in other words KUKA robocoaster technology. This propelled you though Hogwarts, past a fire breathing dragon and into Aragog's lair, by the way Aragog is the spider in Harry Potter.

Moving on from the rides, the shows were all magical as well. We went and watched a Fear Factor show, if you can't remember the program, Fear Factor was an old TV show where contestants were challenged to face their fears. The show was pretty amazing as contestants had to do some cool looking stunts like fall off a cliff, with a harness of course. We also went to watch a pet show where we saw the dog from Men In Black as well as other famous pets used in films. Last but not least, one evening before we were leaving the park, parade floats came around with all the dressed up characters from the movies such as the Simpsons, Dora The Explorer, Shrek and SpongeBob Squarepants, he lives under the sea by the way. Overall, the shows were pretty awesome, as an American would say.

"We saw a lot of thunder."

In terms of thunder, during the second week in Orlando, it thundered everyday around 4pm. This didn't spoil our fun though as we were used to it, plus I got some fantastic images of some lightning strikes. We visited Busch Gardens, a local zoo and theme park and spent half the day sheltering from a storm after it decided to thunder, whilst we had an "all you can eat BBQ" at a water park one afternoon as it was forced to shut due to thunderstorms. We knew thunderstorms were going to be part of our holiday though, so we were prepared but we never let it ruin our holiday.

Last, but not least on our Orlando trip, we visited a Mall, in other words it was called the Mall At Malina. I was hoping this Mall played down to a stereotypical Mall In America. Unfortunately, this Mall was very similar to all the shopping centres in the UK, it had designer shop, after designer shop. I mean who can afford to buy this stuff. One posh shop it did have was an Apple store. The second time we visited my Sister's phone broke and I wanted an Apple Watch so we spent about three hours of our holiday in the Apple Store. That was just half the story though; it took us two hours to find it as we decided to take a bus. We got off at the wrong stop so we had to ask in Starbucks for someone to call us a taxi, eventually we arrived back at the Mall.

Moving on From Orlando, my next trip to America was slightly different, this was with my Dad, we went to Vegas, baby. Now if I had to compare the two trips, I'd say Vegas gave me more of an American experience. What I mean by that is the "big" juicy burgers, the "huge" wild crowds, as my Grandad says, everything is "bigger" and "better" in America. As Universal Studios is more of a theme park, this was hard to see on my trip as a lot of the places and restaurants we visited were themed around a TV program, whereas in Vegas, it was completely American. That's not to say I didn't enjoy both holidays, I did, no matter what experience I got from them.

Anyway, we flew to Vegas via San Francisco, so technically I've been to San Francisco before, even though it was only for 3 hours. You wouldn't have thought we only had 5 days in Vegas we did a lot, we visited every single hotel on the strip, we went to the Hoover Dam, we visited the Old Downtown, a.k.a Freemont Street and we had a gamble. We did all of this in 5 days, non-stop, we needed another holiday after doing all that but it was an experience I'll never forget.

"Vegas was a jam packed holiday."

Many people say Vegas is a place you should go if you like gambling but what people don't realise is that there is some amazing art in Vegas. Yes, art is all over Vegas, the hotels are incredible, some of them are the size of seven football pitches put together, that's huge. In fact, I went into nearly every hotel in Vegas, yes nearly every hotel I walked around. If I had to choose a favourite, I'd choose all of them, there are so many to choose from, it's so difficult to decide. There's the Venetian, this had a canal running through the hotel, it's built to look like Venice, there's the New York, New York hotel, this has the Statue of Liberty right outside it and a huge rollercoaster going through the building.

Talking about hot weather, I did make my Dad walk from the Mandalay Bay hotel to the Las Vegas Sign in 40 degrees heat. Don't blame me though, I thought it was closer to walk, it looked closer, I could see the sign from the hotel but nobody told me that was half a mile away. It was scorching heat and we got halfway and there was no public transport. It made sense to carry on walking and not turn back, even though we were beginning to look like two identical puddles, after all it was closer to the sign than it was to walk back again to the Mandalay Bay hotel. Eventually, we arrived at the Las Vegas sign, my Dad cried with relief he could finally get a bus back, whilst I was more excited to actually see the Vegas sign, yes it was the Vegas sign in real life.

Another hotel that was really incredible was the Stratosphere Hotel. We climbed, well got the lift up to the top of the hotel which was the height of the London Eye three times over. At the top of the lift we were greeted to an incredible view of the strip. I even decided to get seated on one of the highest and most daring rides in the world. With just a harness for protection, the ride sent you out to look face down at the ground. If you're afraid of heights I do not recommend you go on this ride. Luckily I wasn't afraid of heights and I really enjoyed the thrill it gave me. Deep down I knew the ride was 100% safe, there was no way on earth the ride could come loose, they wouldn't let you on the ride in the first place. I mean, why do people get scared of falling of a ride?, if they weren't 100% safe, they wouldn't let you on it. One thing that was incredible In Vegas was the Bellagio Fountains. These were a series of fountains that danced to music with such amazing timing. At night these fountains came alive, you could literally watch them dancing all night, they are so beautiful.

Now my third and final holiday with my Dad was on a large, a very, very large ship last October. In other words we went on a cruise around the Mediterranean. Now 2 years ago, I would have never even considered going on a cruise, I'd say it was "for old people" and that you have to "dress up smart" all the time. The truth is, yes you do and there are a lot of older people on the cruise but there are so many pluses for young people too. For starters, the unlimited alcohol, the free food and the excitement of waking up to new destination, every single morning. That's why you should go on a cruise, they are amazing, the theatre shows are incredible and are performed to a West End standard. The food is extremely well cooked, plus you get a three course a la carte meal every night.

"It was a very, very large cruise ship."

Anyway, we visited six countries, yes SIX countries whilst on our very big ship, Corsica, a French island just by Italy, Rome, Florence, Pisa, Monte Carlo, Monaco and Ibiza. Now that's a lot of countries and it was, in fact it tired us completely out. Next time, I go on a cruise. I think we'll consider limiting the number of excursions we do as it can get very tiring visiting every single country all at once. If I had to choose a favourite city I'd choose Florence, it really is a city of art, some of the buildings are incredible.

THOUGHTS DIARY

So, thoughts, thoughts are key to understanding your experience and your life. So I thought what better way for you to get to know me than publish my thoughts in this book. Here's a series of thoughts I had whilst in a mental health hospital and suffering from a "psychotic episode" as well as thoughts I've had whilst being out of hospital.

23rd May – 31st May 2020

"Loved the gym, I met a nurse who believes I can enter the Paralympics 5,000 metres."

"I'm getting better, all the nurses seem to see a huge difference in me."

"My mum brought me some cookies and lemon cake, mmm."

"I waved to my Mum in the window, I love waving, I know I'll see her soon. Harry and Thomas were their too."

"Played Fifa, felt a little unsecure around the other patient."

"Coloured a deer in this morning, it was really colourful."

"Might be doing some cooking tomorrow, that sounds exciting."

Monday 1st June

"Another good day being Monday, I started the day focusing on my book, then doing some colouring before relaxing and watching some TV on my bed."

Tuesday 2nd June

"Had my ward round meeting earlier today, it went well and I potentially could have a discharge meeting next Tuesday. I'm not getting my hopes up too much though. Had the usual gym session and went for an evening run in the garden."

Wednesday 3rd June

"Today's been a good day, I met my Mum and my sister and we went for a walk, despite the drizzling rain. We had a picnic, it was the best picnic ever as we had chocolate pie and put a picnic blanket over the bench to make it more scenic. I've been to the gym too and I'm now writing this blog at 3pm in the afternoon."

Thursday 4th June

"Really struggling today in managing my feelings, I'm feeling like I just want to lie down and sleep. I'm continually challenging myself though and I know it's important to take things slowly before taking the next step of moving home."

Friday 5th June

"Wrote 11,000 words of my book, it's slowly getting written. I think I just need to go and write my book and have a lie down when I need to have a lie down."

Saturday 6th June

"I think keeping busy is key for me, not too busy but busy enough to take my mind of things."

Sunday 7th June

"Not motivated whatsoever but I'm feeling good now."

Monday 8th June

"I had a difficult morning but I'm feeling much better now as it's the afternoon, I really think I'll be out this mental health hospital tomorrow but I just need to take one day as it comes. A lot of the nurses have said I will

be out but I'm not sure, just going to play everything by ear, not expecting anything."

Tuesday 9th June

"I'm going home today, I know it will get easier from now on because I have my home comforts."

Wednesday 10th June – Wednesday 17th June

"Things have gone okay so far, I have a project which is this book to complete, I've ran a 6 mile run this morning so my running is coming back again. I just really need to stop worrying about not being able to focus on stuff. I just need to relax as much as possible at home and gradually I'll get better. My brain is broken, it needs time to heal."

Thursday 18th June – Wednesday 24th June

"I'm feeling like I'm getting better. I still feel like I can't focus for long on things but slowly I'm becoming myself again."

Thursday 25th June – Tuesday 30th June

"I'm dreading the mornings, getting up is proving to be really difficult but I get up, I go for a run, I do the things I want to do but it's a struggle. I think I'm having a little bit of depression, which is perfectly normal after everything I've been through."

Wednesday 1st July

"It's now July and I've been out of hospital for nearly 4 weeks. It's feels like a lifetime though, I keep getting a feeling of dread when I wake up in the morning, I simply do not want to get up."

"Every time I try and do a task in the day, all I can think about is the end of the day."

" I'm trying so hard to keep myself busy. Most of the days I simply cannot be bothered to think about things, I just want to lie down and sleep."

Thursday 2nd July

"This was going to be a long day as I had 2 video calls, one was with my art group and the other was with MIND."

"I started the day with another 5k run, I got up a bit earlier so I wasn't late for my first video call and managed to finish the run."

"I had my first video call with a group of people who have experienced psychosis. The group is called Artscape and they are part of a unit who help with the early *prevention of psychosis. I really enjoyed my time with the art group."*

Friday 3rd July

"I started the day with a 3 mile run. After my run, I was thinking of something to do and then I realised I could mow the lawn."

"Mowing the lawn isn't as simply as it sounds, there is a lot of grass and it could go everywhere so I have to be cautious."

"My Care Coordinator, CARL came to visit in the afternoon. CARL's such a nice man and he's going to help me through my psychosis recovery."

Saturday 4th July

"Now, Saturday's are usually my favourite days of the week, this Saturday I wasn't particularly excited about as I had to go to my Dads. Now I love going to my Dads but the thing is, I'm always having to think of something to do whilst I'm there, I just want to sit down on my bed and not think about anything."

"When I go to my Dads I feel like I'm expected to think about stuff all the time, I can't simply go and lay on my bed and think about nothing like I can do at my Mums."

" I got to my Dads and we sat down and watched Frozen 2, this was a good film, although I don't think it's target market was two grown men with the average age of 30."

Sunday 5th July

"I spent Sunday at my Dads where we did everything you could possibly name under the sun. We started the day eating scrambled egg on toast, Dad put cheese in the egg though which made it taste cheesy but nice at the same time. I then proposed to ride the bike for an hour in the living room, that quickly changed to 30 minutes when I realised my bum would really, really start to ache and go very, very numb."

"After a bit of painful bike riding, we did some cooking, I cooked a carrot cake with my Dad. I love carrot cake, my sister and brothers aren't so keen on it though, I think the prospect of carrot and cake, a.k.a veg and cake isn't very appealing to many people."

"For lunch we had roast pork with crackling, plus an apple tart tartin for pudding, this was nice. I hadn't had a roast for a while."

Monday 6th July

"Slowing things down a bit today as I'm knackered from the weekend. I did a lot with my Dad and it was quite difficult for me mentally to keep up."

"I just feel like I have no motivation whatsoever which is really annoying considering how much motivation I used to have. I used to be up at 6.30am, then I used to run a half marathon, eat healthily and literally blast my way through the day."

Tuesday 7th July

"Tuesday was very much a slow day again. I spent most of the day in bed but I'm getting there. I'm slowly feeling more alert as my new medication is kicking in. Olanzapine is making me really sleepy at the minute but I'm getting through the days."

Wednesday 8th July

"It was lovely meeting the guys from MIND for the first time today. It was so amazing to meet Richard, Kirsty, Alex and Ian in person rather than virtually using Zoom. We went to a PUB, yes a PUB."

Thursday 9th July

"Thursday's are busy days and this was no exception. I had two online video calls, the first one being my Artscape call. "

"I had my second call this afternoon, this time it was with the people from MIND. This week, it was Desert Island Discs. We had to make an important decision, if we were stranded on a desert island with only one song and a luxury item, what would we choose?"

Friday 10th July

"Well, fish and chip Friday has finally arrived. I love Fridays, they are the end of the week, a chance to let your hair down and relax."

"My Care Coordinator came round to visit today. I cut out some pieces of paper with signs of psychosis I experienced in hospital. We went through the signs as part of my re-lapse prevention work and made a note of the signs and symptoms I experienced in hospital. If I ever have any of these signs I must let my Mum or CARL know."

Saturday 11th July

"Visited my Sister's house today, we went there for an hour. I was so jealous when they said they were off to TGI Fridays to eat."

Sunday 12th July

"It was a busy visit to my Dad's house today. We stopped by my Nan's initially where it was lovely to be able to go inside my Nans house and talk to them about stuff we always used to talk to them about, like football, cricket and my car."

"We even treated ourselves to a bit of chocolate cake at 11am, mmm, I love chocolate, in fact in hospital I eat a plate full of cake pops in one go, now before you ask, that is a lot of cake and chocolate at once."

Monday 13th July

"I've been sleeping a lot recently; today I spent a lot of the day asleep or relaxing in bed. As my Mum's said beforehand, the brain is connected to your body, if you feel you need sleep you must go to rest and recover, so that's exactly what I did."

"I'm writing this book now, but I'm not pushing myself, If I feel I've written enough for one day I will stop and my book writing will resume whenever I feel like it."

Tuesday 14th July

"I got a bit of art work completed as well as a bit of my book. It's always good to pace myself and do what I can do."

Wednesday 15th July

"I met with the guys and gals from MIND again today. This week we went to, yes another PUB."

Thursday 16th July

"It's starting to feel like everything's coming together, slowly I'm starting to find it easier to think. I still need to take things slowly; all it takes is one day to bring me down again. That feeling of dread is slowly merging into a feeling of just needing to relax. I had my two video calls today as well, one being my Artscape one and the other my MIND call."

Friday 17th July

"Guess what I had for tea? Fish and Chips of course, it was Friday again and Friday's obviously mean only one thing, Fish and Chips."

"CARL came to visit too and we put together a timeline of my psychosis events. This allowed us to establish the early warning signs so if I were to get ill again we know how to stop it."

Saturday 18th July

"I'm starting to love walking, we went on a walk around Bodicote. We walked through all sorts of fields, one with big, long, sweetcorn looking stalks, one with potato looking plants and one with broad beans. Bodicote brings back a lot of memories when I was younger, we used to walk around there whilst my Nan was babysitting us as children. There was an annual duck racing competition that was held around the grounds of Bodicote too which we used to go too. The walk brought back a lot of memories which I will treasure forever."

Sunday 19th July

"It was BBQ weather, so we went to my sister's for a BBQ. We had sausages, burgers (we didn't forget to add cheese and toast the bun either), chicken alongside all the works of a BBQ."

Monday 20th July

"I start every day with a walk and that's what I did today. I'm not alone on my walk either, I wake up my Mum every morning and we go for a walk together. That way she gets up early, I get up early and we all start the day off bright."

Tuesday 21st July

"As usual Tuesday started with a struggle to get up but it soon changed when I got my book out. When I write this book I seem to drift away from the troubles of society and my thinking and just focus on the pages and the words of this book."

Wednesday 22nd July

"Been a busy day once again, I met with the people from MIND. Guess what, we went to another PUB. Unfortunately, my MUM got stung by a wasp just under here eye."

Thursday 23rd July

"MIND and Artscape both went ahead again. This week we had to name our favourite children's TV show from our childhood. I chose Bernard's Watch as my favourite, it's one of those programs where you can imagine what life would be like if that were to happen. For example, if I were to stop time I could do anything and get away with it, it would be an amazing experience, I just wish a watch existed."

Friday 24th July

"I only went and fell off my bike didn't I, I was only a 6 mile bike ride with my Mum but the water bottle fell off my bike leading me to lose my balance."

Saturday 25th July

"Jack and Charlotte came over to our house and we moved a lot of furniture around. The house looks so stuffed full of furniture at the minute; it's making me feel a bit anxious. I want to clear the furniture out but my Mum wants to keep a lot of it to sell it. I know the furniture will clear eventually."

Sunday 26th July

"I hadn't been to tea at my Nans in ages. I used to go every Wednesday before taking a trip to the gym. Back then I was really pushing myself, I used to really push hard on the treadmill which could have been a factor in my psychotic episode. Now I just wish I spent more time with my Nan rather than rushing off to the gym straight after tea."

Monday 27th July

"It took ages but I finally downloaded Grand Theft Auto to play on my PlayStation. I'm going to start focusing on gaming and playing video games at night rather than in the evening, it might help me relax more as watching TV at the minute is proving to be rather a challenge. "

Tuesday 28th July

"I had a go at Grand Theft Auto this afternoon and it was a good game. The problem is though, I've already played a lot of the game so I know what's going to happen. I think I'll treat myself to another game at a later date. I also snuck upstairs and listened to the "Best Of The West End" on BBC Radio 2. I love musical songs, they are so uplifting and really make you feel good, I think I need to listen to more of them."

Wednesday 29th July

"It was lovely meeting for a picnic in People's Park today, the whole gang was there, Kirsty, Richard, Jamie, Alex and co. We made cheese and pickle sandwiches which were delicious. I hope to have a picnic some time again soon."

Thursday 30th July

"We played Charades during my MIND call today. It was something different and it really got my acting side going again. I did the charade 'Up' which was easy really, all I had to do was point upwards."

Friday 31st July

"It's the last day of July. Today's been a hot day and I've been sweating everywhere. I hate sweating, it really makes your clothes wet which means you can't wear them the next day."

ONE YEAR LATER

Well, it's been a year since I've been out of hospital and what a year it's been. I'm slowly recovering but there have been some major changes in my life which I want to address in one last chapter. It's taken me over a year to get this book published so I feel it's important to not ignore the changes which are taking place in my life and reflect on each and every one of them.

"Now's the time to reflect"

The first change is that sadly after seven and a half years, I've left my job as a Social Media Executive. I was going back to work using a phased structure but the pressure, stress and anxiety of working in such an ever changing environment took its toll on me and so I had to leave my role. I'm not looking at this event as a failure though; I'm looking at it as a stepping stone to better things. See, I was waking up every morning with a huge dread feeling, I really didn't want to spend my days sat at a computer, I struggle to use the computer too, well it's mainly screens I really struggle with, for example I hate watching TV. This dread feeling was getting worse and worse and so I felt it was best to leave my role and look into other options.

One thing I have done to get me back into the working zone is start at Bridewell Organic Gardens. Bridewell is a mental health garden and was set up to help people who've been through and are recovering from severe mental health difficulties. When I first went for my introductory meeting with Bridewell I was very nervous, one thing that kept playing on my mind was the parking as I was unsure on how much there would be. Parking itself is one thing that lets me down on the driving scene. I always worry about where to park as I struggle to fit into tight spaces. When I say "struggle" I mean I panic that I'll hit another car when I have to park close to another one. Anyway, the parking was good at Bridewell and I'm glad to say that I've been going since that day I had my introductory meeting once a week.

"It's such a magical place."

Every time I visit Bridewell, it feels so magical. The garden itself is beautiful and they have all sorts of plants, fruits and vegetables. They even have their own chicken pen and chickens to go along with the garden. My day at Bridewell usually starts with a morning briefing with a cup of coffee, well I have squash as I don't like hot drinks. After drinking my squash I choose my morning activity, the activities are written down on a whiteboard for you to choose from, there's all sorts of things to get up to, from pot washing to cutting the old man's beard to picking up apples along the Avenue. The garden itself has different names, for example you may have noticed I called a part of the garden "The Avenue". This is the part of the garden where the apples are growing and it looks amazing to walk up and down it. There's other parts of the garden too, but I'm not too sure on their names as I'm quite new to them.

"I've never done gardening before."

Now I've never done gardening so this was something completely new to me but I'm glad to say I enjoyed it. Last week, I used a saw and hammer and made kindle wood out of old wood pallets. I've never used a saw or hammer in my life but I found it incredibly useful learning how to use the tools. It also felt a bit dangerous using the saw, I like danger, there's something about knowing how the tool you're using could cut your finger or arm off. It's the same with fire, in fact we have a fire going at Bridewell, we've even made Bonfire's in the past.

Moving away from Bridewell, I had a few weeks where I applied for jobs to get back in the working scene. In fact,

I didn't just apply for jobs I received four, yes four different interviews. Having Aspergers means interviews are a pretty scary thing to do. I struggle to mainly answer the questions in an interview scene, the words sometimes come out stuttered and I sometimes can't think of anything to say. You'll be glad to hear that I'm having interview skills training with someone at Bridewell though. They're helping me process where I want to go in my career next whilst helping me answer questions I may be asked in an interview scene.

Anyway, going back to my interviews I had, they were scary but I warned them in advanced that I had Aspergers, this way they knew I would struggle and knew how I'd be during the interview. The first interview was for Tescos and it was on a Saturday, I was the only one dressed smart. There was another boy in the interview room with me, he was wearing a t-shirt and tracksuit bottoms whilst I was in a shirt and trousers. The questions were pretty generic and basic but the simplicity of the questions made them difficult to answer.

The other interviews I attended were for Royal Mail, HMV and Sainsburys. These interviews were more or less very similar to each other. They asked similar questions such as "Tell me about yourself" and went through my CV.

"Tesco's offered me a job."

After attending my interviews, Tesco's offered me a temporary position for Christmas. I attended the induction and had plans to start but I felt it was too much in the end. I started crying to my Mum and she was so supportive, she knew I wasn't ready to start work as she could see me becoming more and more anxious. So I decided I wasn't ready and rang Tesco up to let them know I wouldn't be starting.

It's Christmas now and I'm just focusing on the things that I have at the minute. It's obvious, but if you focus on the things you have right now you appreciate them much, much more. Looking at my life right now, I go to Bridewell each week, I meet my MIND friends for lunch, I go to MIND, I go on a walk every Friday, I'm writing this book, I've signed up for a new challenge to run 31 miles during the run up to Christmas, I'm even in a pantomime this year!

"I'm focusing on the things I have."

Yes, you heard right, I'm in a pantomime this year, I actually joined a drama group in my local village. It was difficult joining a new group especially when I didn't know anyone, but I did it and that's something I should be proud of. I remember when I used to be scared of going into a shop, but I overcome it and I'm becoming more and more confident to do the things I've always found tough due to my Aspergers.

"A growth mindset is crucial."

Interestingly, I attended an insightful MIND course yesterday. They discussed the difference between a growth and a fixed mindset. To put it simply, a fixed mindset is a mindset that doesn't change and believes things won't change no matter how hard they try whilst a growth mindset is a mindset that believes they can do something, that anything is possible. This book itself is a fantastic example of how I demonstrate a growth mindset. My attitude to battling with Aspergers is a clear example of a growth mindset. I feel that anyone with Aspergers or autism for that matter has a growth mindset as they are continually having to battle new ways of dealing with life. Having a growth mindset is something so important especially if you have Aspergers as if you give and except that you can't do something you won't achieve anything. As I said at the start of this book there are so many famous people, Einstein and Newton for example, who've been diagnosed with Aspergers. They are all examples of people with a growth mindset. I thoroughly believe that those with Aspergers can do anything just as I have done, if you put your mind to it.

Printed in Great Britain
by Amazon